CIMA Official Terminology
2005 Edition

The Chartered Institute of Management Accountants

ELSEVIER

AMSTERDAM • BOSTON • HEIDELBERG • LONDON
NEW YORK • OXFORD • PARIS • SAN DIEGO
SAN FRANCISCO • SINGAPORE • SYDNEY • TOKYO

CIMA Publishing is an imprint of Elsevier

CIMA
PUBLISHING

CIMA Publishing
An imprint of Elsevier
Linacre House, Jordan Hill, Oxford OX2 8DP
30 Corporate Drive, Burlington, MA 01803

First published 1982
Reprinted (with amendments) January 1984
Reprinted September 1984
Reprinted June 1987
Revised 1991, 1996, 2000
This revised and updated edition published 2005

British Library Cataloguing in Publication Data
A catalogue record for this book is available from the British Library

Library of Congress Cataloguing in Publication Data
A catalogue record for this book is available from the Library of Congress

ISBN-10   0-7506-8627-X
ISBN-13   978-0-7506-6827-9

For information on all CIMA Publishing Publications visit
our website at www.cimapublishing.com

Typeset by Integra Software Services Pvt. Ltd, Pondicherry, India
www.integra-india.com

Transferred to Digital Printing in 2011

Contents

Introduction

The relevance of this quote can be appreciated when we consider the timing of this new edition of the *CIMA Official Terminology*. Since the last edition was prepared in 2000, a highly significant milestone has been reached for financial reporting, with the improvements to, and consequent widespread acceptance of, a set of globally acceptable international accounting standards. In response to this, and other developments which have increased the internationalisation of the profession, CIMA's syllabus has examined students on the international accounting standards regime since May 2005. This has had consequences for the content of this terminology, discussed under *Scope* below.

This introduction explains how the terminology is structured, the conventions we have followed, and how to get the most from it. It also contains CIMA's definitions of Management Accounting, and the work of the Chartered Management Accountant. A Chartered Management Accountant is an accountant who has gained the CIMA professional qualification and is either an associate or fellow member of the Institute, denoted by the letters ACMA or FCMA after their name. When we consider the nature of the work of the management accountant, and the priority it gives to communication with management, the importance of an authoritative terminology such as this is evident.

Purpose

The purpose of this book is to introduce and explain to readers, important terms relevant to the work of the management accountant. It is essential reading for those studying any papers of the CIMA Certificate in Business Accounting or the CIMA professional qualification, enabling them to find a definition quickly without resorting to a textbook. *Official Terminology* is also recommended for professional accountants in business who have undertaken, or are likely to undertake, fresh responsibilities and who therefore need to familiarise themselves with new terms or concepts, from an authoritative source.

Scope and international perspective

The title of this publication has changed from that used in previous editions '*Management Accounting Official Terminology*' to '*CIMA Official Terminology*'. The change is intended to show that the scope of this text is more than just management accounting (a broad discipline in itself) but includes some of the broader range of those activities potentially required of CIMA members and other professional accountants in business.

This is a text primarily for those currently engaged in management accounting and related fields. Not all entries in the *Official Terminology* will be fully comprehensible to the layperson; but this text is suitable for thousands of CIMA students and members who form its global audience. Note that due to the increasing internationalisation of the discipline, we have added a number of recognised international terms, for example 'inventories', 'receivables' and 'income statement' as well as their respective equivalents 'stock', 'debtors' and 'profit and loss account' which are, at present, still widely used in the UK and many other countries.

As with all such publications, we were limited by space and had to be discriminating about the terms we included. However, due to the various transitions through which ethical, reporting and auditing regimes are passing (the internationalisation of the profession noted in the opening paragraph); many terms included in this edition are new, or have a limited lifespan, and are included in parallel with the terms they are replacing or to which they are equivalents. Thus, in respect of narrative reporting, we include definitions for not only *Operating and Financial Review (UK)*, but also *Management's Discussion and Analysis (USA)*. Where terms are only applicable to a single country, these are indicated by a reference to the UK or US, as appropriate. Where no such indication is given, assume the terms are internationally accepted.

In common with the conventions of most management accounting textbooks, and the scope of manufacturing on an international scale, several manufacturing examples are used in this Official Terminology.

Organisation of terms

Terms are listed alphabetically on pages 104 to 114. What makes the *Official Terminology* particularly useful is that terms are also grouped thematically. Four key areas have a chapter dedicated to each, which defines the relationships between relevant terms, and illustrates important concepts which are necessary to understand the topic. More than a simple dictionary, not quite a textbook, the *Official Terminology* serves to bridge the gap between the two.

The nature of the *Official Terminology* affects how we have organised the terms. For example, there are many different kinds of risk, grouped into several categories such as market risks, or financial risks. Common to all risks however, is the need for a process to understand and manage them. It is more informative therefore to consider risk terms as a group within one chapter. Readers will find specific terms, for example, currency risk or reputation risk under C and R respectively in the Index, which will refer them to the relevant pages within Chapter Two.

The *Official Terminology* lists those UK and International Accounting Standards and Financial Reporting Standards extant at the time of publication in the Appendices.

The definition of Management Accounting

Management accounting is the application of the principles of accounting and financial management to create, protect, preserve and increase value for the stakeholders of for-profit and not-for-profit enterprises in the public and private sectors.

Management accounting is an integral part of management. It requires the identification, generation, presentation, interpretation and use of relevant information to:

- Inform strategic decisions and formulate business strategy
- Plan long, medium and short-run operations
- Determine capital structure and fund that structure
- Design reward strategies for executives and shareholders
- Inform operational decisions
- Control operations and ensure the efficient use of resources
- Measure and report financial and non-financial performance to management and other stakeholders
- Safeguard tangible and intangible assets
- Implement corporate governance procedures, risk management and internal controls

The work of the Chartered Management Accountant

Chartered Management Accountants help organisations establish viable strategies and convert them into profit (in a commercial context) or into value for money (in a not-for-profit context). To achieve this they work as an integral part of multi-skilled management teams in carrying out the:

- Formulation of policy and setting of corporate objectives;
- Formulation of strategic plans derived from corporate objectives;

- Formulation of shorter-term operational plans;
- Acquisition and use of finance;
- Design of systems, recording of events and transactions and management of information systems;
- Generation, communication and interpretation of financial and operating information for management and other stakeholders;
- Provision of specific information and analysis on which decisions are based;
- Monitoring of outcomes against plans and other benchmarks and the initiation of responsive action for performance improvement;
- Derivation of performance measures and benchmarks, financial and non-financial, quantitative and qualitative, for monitoring and control; and
- Improvement of business systems and processes through risk management and internal audit review.

Through these forward-looking roles and by application of their expert skills management accountants help organisations improve their performance, security, growth and competitiveness in an ever more demanding environment.

Disclaimer

Acknowledgements

The production of the 2005 edition of the CIMA Official Terminology would not have been possible without the help and advice of a number of contributors.

Special thanks go to the working party for their expertise, determination and patience; Kim Ansell (CIMA), Professor David Dugdale (University of Bristol), David Harris (CIMA), David Kyle (Sheffield Hallam University), Louise Ross (CIMA), Danka Starovic (CIMA), Joan Toon (PJ Partnership), Kate Wilcox (CIMA) and, in particular, to the Chair, Professor Falconer Mitchell (University of Edinburgh). Additional support was provided by Dr Beat Reber (Nottingham University).

Thanks also go to CIMA's Technical department, particularly Richard Mallett and Nick Topazio for their invaluable contribution.

The work was improved with the objective review of the content provided by CIMA's Technical Committee and CIMA's Research & Development Group, as well as individual review by Professor Colin Drury, Professor Christine Helliar, Maurice Lalley and Jim Moyes.

Finally, thanks go to those who responded during the consultation process, providing recommendations for the 2005 edition of the CIMA Official Terminology.

Foreword

It is a hardly an exaggeration to say that change is ever-present in the financial world, but the pace of change has been particularly intense in the last few years.

Since the last edition of the *Official Terminology* was published, accountants and accounting practices across the globe have rarely left the headlines – and not always for the right reasons. From the corporate governance scandals and new legislation created in their wake, to the introduction of International Financial Reporting Standards, the content of accounting and its environment have changed substantially.

Of course, CIMA itself has been changing too. We have an evolving syllabus and practice mandatory continuing professional development (CPD) in accordance with the International Federation of Accountants' *International Education Standard for Professional Accountants*.

This revised Official Terminology is therefore designed to reflect contemporary management accounting changes and because the profession is never static we will, of course, continue to revise and update the *Official Terminology* in the future.

The boundaries of management accounting are by no means clear-cut so a short book such as this one will not include everything. However, it defines many useful terms in straightforward language and, in a number of cases, provides examples to show how they are used.

Like its predecessors, this edition is intended to be a reference work for CIMA students and members as well as anyone who needs to have an understanding of management accounting. It is the essential vocabulary of the profession.

CIMA Council
October 2005

Management Accounting

abnormal gain   Improvement on the accepted or normal level of loss associated with a production activity. It is isolated as a period entry rather than as an adjustment to product cost.

abnormal loss   Any loss in excess of the normal loss allowance. It is isolated as a period entry rather than as a component of product cost.

absorbed overhead   Overhead attached to products or services by means of an absorption rate, or rates.
under- or over-absorbed overhead   The difference between overhead incurred and overhead absorbed, using an estimated rate, in a given period.
   If overhead absorbed is less than that incurred there is under-absorption, if overhead absorbed is more than that incurred there is over-absorption. Over- and under-absorptions are treated as period cost adjustments. *See* Figure 1.1.

absorption rate   *See* overhead absorption rate.

accounting manual   Collection of accounting instructions governing the responsibilities of persons, and the procedures, forms and records relating to the preparation and use of accounting data. There can be separate manuals for the constituent parts of the accounting system, such as a budget manual or cost accounting manual.

accounting period   Time period covered by the accounting statements of an entity. There may be different time periods for different accounting statements, for example management accounts may be

FIGURE 1.1 COST ALLOCATION, APPORTIONMENT AND OVERHEAD ABSORPTION

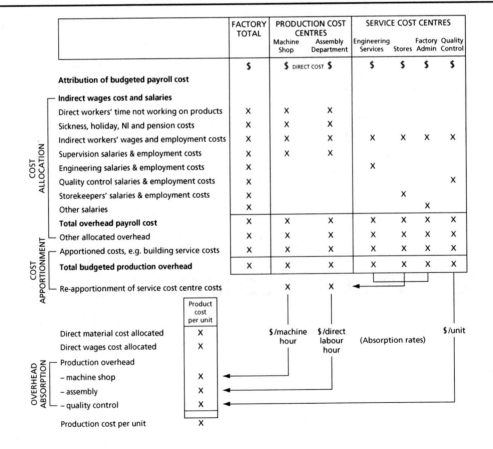

for four- or five-week periods to coincide with a thirteen-week financial accounting period.

accounts, integrated   Set of accounting records that integrates both financial and cost accounts using a common input of data for all accounting purposes.

accounts, interlocking   Set of accounting records where the cost and financial accounts are distinct, the two being kept continuously in agreement by the use of control accounts or reconciled by other means.

activities, hierarchy of   Classification of activities by level of organisation, for example unit, batch, product sustaining and facility sustaining.

activity, batch level   Activity (such as setting-up machines) where volume varies directly with the number of batches of output but is independent of the number of units in a batch. *See* activities, hierarchy of.

activity cost pool   Aggregation of all costs related to a specific activity.

activity driver   Transaction that causes an activity. For example, receipt of a sales order sets in train the order processing activity.

activity driver analysis   Identification and evaluation of the activity drivers used to trace the cost of activities to cost objects.

activity, facility sustaining   Activity undertaken to support the organisation as a whole, and which cannot be logically linked to individual units of output. Accounting is a facility sustaining activity. *See* activities, hierarchy of.

activity, product sustaining   Activity undertaken to develop or sustain a product (or service). Product sustaining costs are linked to the number of products or services, not to the number of units produced.

activity-based budgeting   Method of budgeting based on an activity framework and utilising cost driver data in the budget setting and variance feedback processes.

activity-based costing (ABC)   Approach to the costing and monitoring of activities which involves tracing resource consumption and costing final outputs. Resources are assigned to activities, and activities to cost objects based on consumption estimates. The latter utilise cost drivers to attach activity costs to outputs. *See* Figure 1.2.

activity-based costing, time-driven (time-driven ABC)   Approach to ABC based on the time required for each unit activity. The method avoids the use of interviews with operating managers in order to estimate percentage of time spent on different areas of work. It is claimed that "time-driven ABC" based on "time per transactional activity"

FIGURE 1.2 THE FRAMEWORK OF ACTIVITY-BASED COSTING

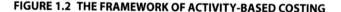

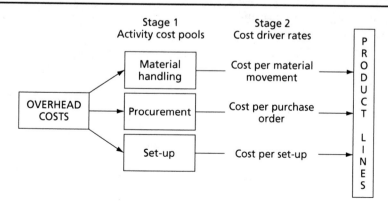

is simpler to install and update and can highlight unused capacity.

activity-based management (ABM)
operational ABM   Actions, based on activity driver analysis, that increase efficiency, lower costs and/or improve asset utilisation.
strategic ABM   Actions, based on activity-based cost analysis, that aim to change the demand for activities so as to improve profitability.

allocate   To assign a whole item of cost, or of revenue, to a single cost unit, centre, account or time period. In the US, "allocate" does not have this precise meaning, it is used more generally to refer to the whole process of overhead apportionment, allocation and absorption. *See* Figure 1.1.

apportion   To spread indirect revenues or costs over two or more cost units, centres, accounts or time periods. This may also be referred to as "indirect allocation".
re-apportion   The re-spread of costs apportioned to service departments to production departments. *See* Figure 1.1

apportionment basis   Physical or financial unit used to apportion costs to cost centres.

batch   Group of similar units which maintains its identity throughout one or more stages of production and is treated as a cost unit.

behavioural implications, accounting
Ways in which people affect, and are affected by, the creation, existence and use of accounting information. For example, *see* budgeting, behavioural aspects and consequences.

bill of materials   Detailed specification, for each product, of the subassemblies, components and materials required, distinguishing items purchased externally from those manufactured in-house.

bottleneck   Facility that has lower capacity than prior or subsequent facilities and

restricts output based on current capacity. *See* theory of constraints, throughput.

breakeven chart   Chart that indicates approximate profit or loss at different levels of sales volume within a limited range. For examples of conventional breakeven charts under different cost structures, *see* Figures 1.3 and 1.4.

FIGURE 1.3 CONVENTIONAL BREAKEVEN CHART I

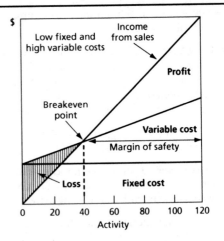

FIGURE 1.4 CONVENTIONAL BREAKEVEN CHART II

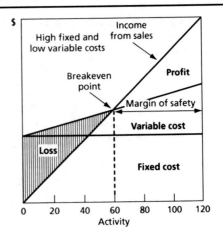

Figure 1.5 shows a contribution breakeven chart and Figure 1.6 a profit–volume chart.

breakeven point   Level of activity at which there is neither profit nor loss. It can be ascertained by using a breakeven chart or by calculation. *See* Figures 1.3, 1.4, 1.5, 1.6 and example:

	$
Sales	10,000
Variable costs (e.g. direct materials, direct labour)	6,000
Contribution	4,000
Fixed cost	2,000
Profit	2,000

Number of units sold	1,000
Contribution per unit	$4
Contribution to sales ratio	

$$\frac{\$4,000}{\$10,000} \times 100 = 40\%$$

Number of units to be sold to breakeven

$$\frac{\text{Total fixed cost}}{\text{Contribution per unit}} = \frac{\$2,000}{\$4}$$
$$= \$500 \text{ units}$$

Sales value at breakeven point

$$\frac{\text{Total fixed cost}}{\text{Contribution to sales ratio}} = \frac{\$2,000}{40\%}$$
$$= \$5,000$$

Time to breakeven

$$\frac{\text{Total fixed cost} \times 365}{\text{Total contribution}} = \frac{\$2,000}{\$4,000} \times 365$$
$$= 6 \text{ mth}$$

(assuming that the period is one year, and that the rate of sales is constant within that period)

budget   Quantitative expression of a plan for a defined period of time. It may include planned sales volumes and revenues; resource quantities, costs and expenses; assets, liabilities and cash flows.

budget, cash   Detailed budget of estimated cash inflows and outflows incorporating both revenue and capital items.

budget centre   Section of an entity for which control may be exercised through prepared budgets. It is often a *responsibility centre* where the manager has authority over, and responsibility for, defined costs and (possibly) revenues.

FIGURE 1.5 CONTRIBUTION BREAKEVEN CHART

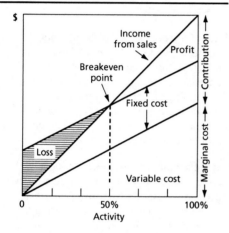

FIGURE 1.6 PROFIT–VOLUME CHART

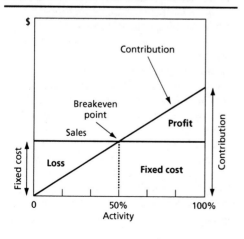

budget cost allowance   Calculated after an accounting period, the cost allowance reflects the actual level of output achieved. Variable costs are flexed in proportion to volume achieved and fixed costs are based on the annual budget.

budget, departmental/functional   Budget of income and/or expenditure applicable to a particular function frequently including sales budget, production cost budget (based on budget production, efficiency and utilisation), purchasing budget, human resources budget, marketing budget, and research and development budget.

budget, fixed   Budget set prior to the control period and not subsequently changed in response to changes in activity, costs or revenues. It may serve as a benchmark in performance evaluation.

budget, flexible   *See* budget flexing.

budget flexing   Flexing variable costs from original budgeted levels to the *allowances* permitted for actual volume achieved while maintaining fixed costs at original budget levels.
   (Variable cost allowance = Ratio of actual volume achieved to budget volume × original budget variable cost)

budget lapsing   Withdrawal of unspent budget allowance due to the expiry of the budget period.

budget, line item   Traditional form of budget layout showing, line by line, the costs of a cost centre analysed by their nature (for example salaries, occupancy, maintenance).

budget manual   Detailed set of guidelines and information about the budget process typically including a calendar of budgetary events, specimen budget forms, a statement of budgetary objectives and desired results, listing of budgetary activities and budget assumptions regarding, for example, inflation and interest rates.

budget, master   Consolidates all subsidiary budgets and is normally comprised of the budgeted profit and loss account, balance sheet and cash flow statement.

budget, operating   Budget of the revenues and expenses expected in a forthcoming accounting period.

budget padding   *See* budget slack.

budget period   Period for which a budget is prepared and used, which may then be subdivided into control periods.

budget, principal factor   Principal budget factor limits the activities of an undertaking. Identification of the principal budget factor is often the starting point in the budget setting process. Often the principal budget factor will be sales demand but it could be production capacity or material supply.

budget purposes   Budgets may help in authorising expenditure, communicating objectives and plans, controlling operations, co-ordinating activities, evaluating performance, planning and rewarding performance. Often, reward systems involve comparison of actual with budgeted performance.

budget, rolling/continuous   Budget continuously updated by adding a further accounting period (month or quarter) when the earliest accounting period has expired. Its use is particularly beneficial where future costs and/or activities cannot be forecast accurately. *See* rolling forecast (Chapter 2).

budget setting processes
bottom-up budgeting   Budgeting process where all budget holders have the opportunity to participate in setting their own budgets.
imposed/top-down budgeting   Budgeting process where budget allowances are set without permitting ultimate budget holders the opportunity to participate in the process.
negotiated budget   Budget in which budget allowances are set largely on the basis of negotiations between budget holders and those to whom they report.
participative budgeting   *See* bottom-up budgeting.

budget slack Intentional overestimation of expenses and/or underestimation of revenue during budget setting. Also known as *budget padding*.

budget virement Authority to apply saving under one budget subhead to meet excesses on others.

budgetary control Master budget, devolved to responsibility centres, allows continuous monitoring of actual results versus budget, either to secure by individual action the budget objectives or to provide a basis for budget revision. *See* control, feedback and control, feedforward.

budgeting, behavioural aspects and consequences
budget constrained style Excessive pressure to achieve budgets that can lead to job-related tension, recriminations, buck-passing and *budget padding*.
non-accounting style Management style that largely ignores budgets and financial information.
profit conscious style Management style that takes account of budgets together with other information and evaluates managerial performance in a flexible manner.
target setting "Tight but achievable" levels are recommended to motivate optimum performance. Too loose a budget can lead to under-achievement as can too tight a budget – and this can also be de-motivating.

budgeting, beyond Idea that companies need to move *beyond budgeting* because of the inherent flaws in budgeting especially when used to set incentive contracts. It is argued that a range of techniques, such as rolling forecasts and market-related targets, can take the place of traditional budgets.

budgeting, incremental Method of budgeting based on the previous budget or actual results, adjusting for known changes and inflation, for example.

budgeting, priority-based Method of budgeting whereby budget requests are accompanied by a statement outlining the changes expected if the prior period budget were increased or decreased by a certain amount or percentage. These changes are prioritised.

budgeting, zero-based Method of budgeting that requires all costs to be specifically justified by the benefits expected.

burden US equivalent of "overhead".

by-product Output of some value produced incidentally while manufacturing the main product. *See* joint products.

capital employed Investment in an entity. In assessing managers it is usually calculated as total assets less current liabilities.
equity capital employed Shareholders' stake in the company. This is important when calculating return to shareholders.

capital expenditure control Procedures for authorising and subsequently monitoring capital expenditure.

capital expenditure proposal/authorisation Formal request for authority to incur capital expenditure usually supported by the case for expenditure in accordance with capital investment appraisal criteria. Levels of authority should be clearly defined with reporting of actual expenditure to the equivalent authority levels.

centre Department, area or function to which costs and/or revenues are charged. *See* Figure 1.1.
budget centre Centre for which an individual budget is drawn up.
cost centre Production or service location, function, activity or item of equipment for which costs are accumulated. *See* Figure 1.1.
investment centre Profit centre with additional responsibilities for capital investment and possibly for financing, and whose performance is measured by its return on investment.

profit centre　Part of a business accountable for both costs and revenues.

responsibility centre　Departmental or organisational function whose performance is the direct responsibility of a specific manager.

revenue centre　Centre devoted to raising revenue with no responsibility for costs, for example a sales centre. Often used in not-for-profit organisations.

service cost centre　Cost centre providing services to other cost centres. When the output of an organisation is a service, rather than goods, an alternative name is normally used, for example support cost centre or utility cost centre. *See* Figure 1.1.

classification　Arrangement of items in logical groups by nature, purpose or responsibility. Classification systems allow financial information to be reported under subjective headings, by cost object or responsibility centre. *See* code.

code　Brief, accurate reference designed to assist classification of items by facilitating entry, collation and analysis. For example, in costing, the first three digits in the composite symbol 211.392 might indicate the nature of the expenditure (*subjective classification*), and the last three digits might indicate the cost centre or cost unit to be charged (*objective classification*).

constraint　Activity, resource or policy that limits the ability to achieve an objective. *See* theory of constraints. In linear programming, constraints define the feasible region within which a solution must lie. *See* linear programming. *See* Figure 1.19.

contribution

(sales value − variable cost of sales) Contribution may be expressed as total contribution, contribution per unit or as a percentage of sales. *See* Figure 1.7.

FIGURE 1.7 BUDGETED TRADING AND PROFIT AND LOSS ACCOUNTS, ABSORPTION COSTING AND MARGINAL COSTING

ABSORPTION COSTING		MARGINAL COSTING		* Note: In an 'actual' absorption costing-based Trading and Profit and Loss Account, production overhead would normally be over- or under-absorbed, due to both cost and activity levels differing from those upon which the budget was based.
Net turnover		**Net turnover**		
Less:		Less:		
Direct Materials		Direct Materials		
Direct Labour		Direct Labour	**Variable Cost of Sales**	
Total Production Overhead	**Production Cost of Sales**	Variable Production Overhead		
	Gross (or Factory) Profit	Variable Selling and Distribution Overhead		An over-absorption occurs when overhead costs absorbed by output exceed the actual costs incurred.
Less:			**Contribution**	
Selling Overhead		Less *fixed costs*:		An under-absorption occurs when the actual costs incurred exceed the overhead costs absorbed by output.
Distribution Overhead		Production Overhead		
Administrative Expenses		Selling Overhead		
		Distribution Overhead		
R&D Cost	**Non-production Overhead**	Administrative Expenses		
	Net Profit before Tax	R&D Cost	**Total Fixed Cost** **Net Profit before Tax**	

control   In management accounting, control usually means ensuring that activities planned and undertaken lead to desired outcomes. *See* control, feedback and control, feedforward.

control, feedback   Measurement of differences between planned outputs and actual outputs achieved, and the modification of subsequent action and/or plans to achieve future required results. Feedback control is an integral part of *budgetary control* and *standard costing systems*. *See* Figure 1.8.

control, feedforward   Forecasting of differences between actual and planned outcomes, and the implementation of action, before the event, to avoid such differences. *See* Figure 1.9.

control, management   All of the processes used by managers to ensure that organisational goals are achieved and procedures adhered to, and that the organisation responds appropriately to changes in its environment.

closed loop system   Control system that includes provision for corrective action, taken on either a *feedforward* or a *feedback* basis. *See* Figures 1.8 and 1.9.

open loop system   Control system that includes no provision for corrective action to be applied to the sequence of activities.

control, operational   Management of daily activities in accordance with strategic and tactical plans. *See* Figure 1.10.

cost   As a noun – The amount of cash or cash equivalent paid or the fair value of other consideration given to acquire an asset at the time of its acquisition or construction (IAS 16).

As a verb – To ascertain the cost of a specified thing or activity. The word *cost* can rarely stand alone and should be qualified as to its nature and limitations.

FIGURE 1.8 A FEEDBACK CONTROL SYSTEM

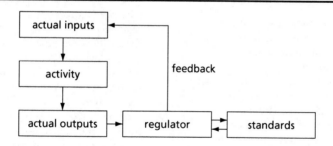

FIGURE 1.9 A FEEDFORWARD CONTROL SYSTEM

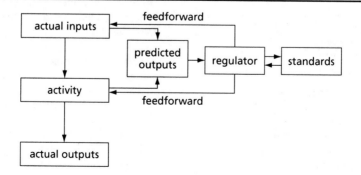

FIGURE 1.10 POLICIES, STRATEGIES, TACTICS AND OPERATIONAL CONTROL

	Industry examples	Services examples
Policies	Produce technically superior products.	Offer low cost services and cultivate customer brand awareness.
Strategy	Spend 15%+ of gross revenue on research and development.	Local price setting to undercut competition. Television advertising to increase brand awareness.
Tactics	Recruit engineers from the best university technology courses.	Price deals to boost volume. Introduce cost reducing technologies.
Operational control	Monitor customer feedback on product performance.	Focus on absolute margin to encourage low price but at high volume. Systematic use of brand awareness feedback.

cost account   Record of expenditure associated with a cost object such as a job, batch, contract or process. Revenue may be credited to the account as, for example, when a process by-product has value.

cost accounting   Gathering of cost information and its attachment to cost objects, the establishment of budgets, standard costs and actual costs of operations, processes, activities or products; and the analysis of variances, profitability or the social use of funds. The use of the term *costing* is not recommended except with a qualifying adjective, for example standard costing.
* batch costing
* continuous operation costing
* contract costing
* job costing
* service/fn costing
* specific order costing
* marginal costing

cost accounting – for cost objects
batch costing   Form of specific order costing where costs are attributed to batches of product (unit costs can be calculated by dividing by the number of products in the batch). *See* figure 1.11.

contract costing   Form of specific order costing where costs are attributed to contracts. *See* Figure 1.11.

job costing   Form of specific order costing where costs are attributed to individual jobs. *See* Figure 1.11.

operations costing   Form of costing where costs are attributed to individual operations within a manufacturing process.

process costing   Form of costing applicable to continuous processes where process costs are attributed to the number of units produced. This may involve estimating the number of equivalent units in stock at the start and end of the period under consideration. *See* Figure 1.11.

specific order costing   Basic cost accounting method applicable if work consists of separately identifiable batches, contracts or jobs. *See* Figure 1.11.

cost accounting – methods
absorption costing   Assigns direct costs *and* all or part of overhead to cost units using one or more overhead absorption rates.
See Figure 1.1.

Sometimes referred to as *full costing* although this is a misnomer if all costs are not attributed to cost units.

FIGURE 1.11 ELEMENTS OF A PRODUCT COSTING SYSTEM

Overall Control System: Budgetary Control				
Product costing system	Specific orders		Continuous operations	
Costing method	Job costing	Batch costing	Contract costing	Continuous operation/ process costing	Service/ function costing
Treatment of fixed production overhead	Absorption or marginal				
Method of cost control	Standard or actual				

direct costing *See* variable costing.
full costing *See* absorption costing.
marginal costing *See* variable costing.
uniform costing Used by several
undertakings, usually in the same industry,
of the same costing methods, principles and
techniques.
variable costing Assigns only variable
costs to cost units while fixed costs are
written off as period costs. *See* Figure 1.7.
Also known as marginal costing and,
especially in the US, as direct costing.

cost allocation/apportionment *See* allocation
and apportionment.

cost, avoidable Specific cost of an activity
or sector of a business that would be
avoided if the activity or sector did not
exist.

cost behaviour Variability of input costs
with activity undertaken. Cost may
increase proportionately with increasing
activity (the usual assumption for a
variable cost), or it may not change with
increased activity (a fixed cost). Some costs
(semi-variable) may have both variable and
fixed elements. Other behaviour is possible,
costs may increase more or less than in
direct proportion, and there may be step
changes in cost, for example. To a large
extent cost behaviour will be dependent
on the timescale assumed. *See* Figures 1.12
and 1.13.

cost classification Arrangement of elements
of cost into logical groups with respect to
their nature (fixed, variable, value adding),
function (production, selling) or use in the
business of the entity.

cost, committed Cost arising from prior
decisions, which cannot, in the short run,
be changed. Committed cost incurrence
often stems from strategic decisions
concerning capacity with resulting
expenditure on plant and facilities. Initial
control of committed costs at the decision
point is through investment appraisal
techniques. *See* commitment accounting.
See Figure 1.14.

cost, common Cost relating to more than
one product or service.

cost, contract Aggregated costs of a single
contract. This usually applies to major
long-term contracts rather than short-
term jobs.

cost control Process that ensures action
is taken if costs exceed a pre-set
allowance (*see* control, feedback) or that
action is taken if costs are forecast to
exceed expected levels (*see* control,
feedforward).

cost, controllable Cost that can be
controlled, typically by a cost, profit or
investment centre manager.

FIGURE 1.12 COST BEHAVIOUR

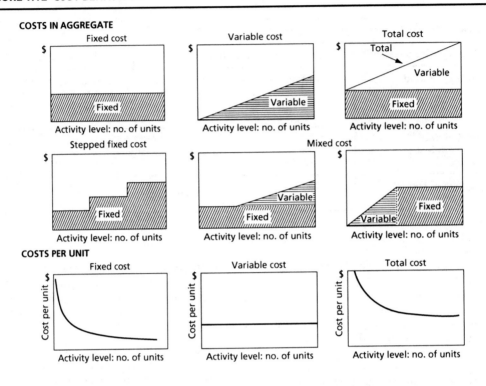

COSTS IN AGGREGATE

COSTS PER UNIT

FIGURE 1.13 ASSESSMENT OF FIXED COST ELEMENT BY THE USE OF A SCATTERGRAPH

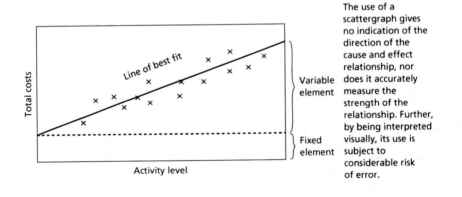

The use of a scattergraph gives no indication of the direction of the cause and effect relationship, nor does it accurately measure the strength of the relationship. Further, by being interpreted visually, its use is subject to considerable risk of error.

cost, conversion   Cost of converting material into finished product, typically including direct labour, direct expense and production overhead.

cost, differential/incremental   Difference in total cost between alternatives. This is calculated to assist decision making.

cost, direct   Expenditure that can be attributed to a specific cost unit, for example material that forms part of the product. *See* Figure 1.1.

cost, discretionary   Cost whose amount within a time period is determined by a decision taken by the appropriate budget

FIGURE 1.14 COMPARISON, OVER THE LIFE OF A PROJECT, OF THE DIFFERENCES BETWEEN COST COMMITMENT AND COST INCURRENCE

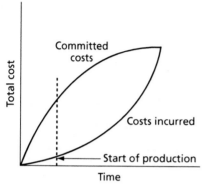

By the start of the production period, most of the costs which will be incurred have already been designed into the product and the selected production technology, and are, once production starts, only marginally susceptible to change.

holder. Marketing, research and training are generally regarded as discretionary costs. Also known as *managed* or *policy* costs.

cost driver　Factor influencing the level of cost. Often used in the context of ABC to denote the factor which links activity resource consumption to product outputs, for example the number of purchase orders would be a cost driver for procurement cost.

cost elements　Constituent parts of costs according to the factors upon which expenditure is incurred, namely material, labour and expenses. *See* Figure 1.15.

cost estimation　Determination of cost behaviour. This can be achieved by engineering methods, analysis of the accounts, use of statistics or by the pooling of expert views.

cost, fixed　Cost incurred for an accounting period, that, within certain output or turnover limits, tends to be unaffected by fluctuations in the levels of activity (output or turnover).

cost, holding　Cost of retaining an asset, generally stock. Holding cost includes the cost of financing the asset in addition to the cost of physical storage.

cost, joint　Cost of a process which results in more than one main product.

cost, long-term variable　All costs are variable in the long run. Full unit costs may be surrogates for long-term variable costs if calculated in a manner which utilises long-term cost drivers, for example activity-based costing.

cost management　Application of management accounting concepts, methods of data collection, analysis and presentation in order to provide the information needed to plan, monitor and control costs.

cost, marginal　Part of the cost of one unit of product or service that would be avoided if the unit were not produced, or that would increase if one extra unit were produced.

cost, notional　Cost used in product evaluation, decision making and performance measurement to reflect the use of resources that have no *actual* (observable) cost. For example, notional interest for internally generated funds or notional rent for use of space.

cost object　For example a product, service, centre, activity, customer or distribution channel in relation to which costs are ascertained.

cost of quality　Difference between the actual cost of producing, selling and supporting products or services and the equivalent costs if there were no failures during production or usage. The cost of quality can be analysed into:
cost of conformance　Cost of achieving specified quality standards.
cost of prevention　Costs incurred prior to or during production in order to prevent substandard or defective products or services from being produced.

FIGURE 1.15 ELEMENTS OF AN ABSORPTION COSTING SYSTEM

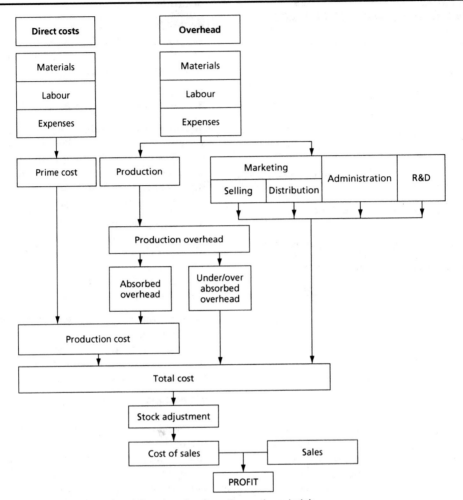

Notes: 1. The above chart is based on the absorption costing principle.
2. In the case of marginal costing, the amount of production overhead absorbed would relate to the variable element only.
3. The relative sizes of the boxes are of no significance.

cost of appraisal   Costs incurred in order to ensure that outputs produced meet required quality standards.

cost of non-conformance   Cost of failure to deliver the required standard of quality.

cost of internal failure   Costs arising from inadequate quality which are identified before the transfer of ownership from supplier to purchaser.

cost of external failure   Cost arising from inadequate quality discovered after the transfer of ownership from supplier to purchaser.

Note: There is no universally accepted definition of quality, which may be assessed on a number of bases, such as conformance to specification, ability to satisfy wants, inclusion of attractive performance/aesthetic attributes, or offering value for money.

cost, opportunity   The value of the benefit sacrificed when one course of action is chosen in preference to an alternative. The opportunity cost is represented by the foregone potential benefit from the best rejected course of action.

cost, overhead/indirect Expenditure on labour, materials or services that cannot be economically identified with a specific saleable cost unit.

The synonymous term *burden* is in common use in the US and in subsidiaries of American companies.

cost, period Cost relating to a time period rather than to the output of products or services.

cost pool Grouping of costs relating to a particular activity in an activity-based costing system.

cost, post-purchase Cost incurred after a capital expenditure decision has been implemented and facilities acquired. May include training, maintenance and the cost of upgrades.

cost, prime Total cost of direct material, direct labour and direct expenses.

cost, product Cost of a finished product built up from its cost elements.

cost, production Prime cost plus absorbed production overhead.

cost, replacement Cost of replacing an asset. This is important in relevant costing because if, for example, material that is in constant use is needed for a product or service, the relevant cost of that material will be its replacement cost. Replacement cost has also been proposed as an alternate to historic cost accounting and it can, therefore, be an important concept with relevance to accounting for inflation or measuring performance where the value of assets is important.

cost, semi-variable Cost containing both fixed and variable components and thus partly affected by a change in the level of activity.

cost, standard Planned unit cost of a product, component or service. The standard cost may be determined on a number of bases (*see* standard). The main uses of standard costs are in performance measurement, control, stock valuation and in the establishment of selling prices. *See* standard product specification.

cost, sunk Cost that has been irreversibly incurred or committed and cannot therefore be considered relevant to a decision. Sunk costs may also be termed *irrecoverable costs.*

cost table Database containing costs associated with production of a product, broken down by function and/or components and sub-assemblies. It incorporates cost changes that would result from possible changes in the input mix.

cost, target Product cost estimate derived by subtracting a desired profit margin from a competitive market price.

cost unit Unit of product or service in relation to which costs are ascertained. *See* Figure 1.16.

cost, variable Cost that varies with a measure of activity.

cost, weighted average Method of unit cost determination, often applied to stocks, in which an average unit cost is calculated, when a new purchase quantity is received:

$$\frac{\text{Cost of opening stock} + \text{Cost of acquisitions}}{\text{Total number of units}}$$

See Figure 1.17.

cost-benefit analysis Comparison between the costs of the resources used plus any other costs imposed by an activity (for example pollution, environmental damage) and the value of the financial and non-financial benefits derived.

costing, backflush Method of costing, associated with a JIT (just-in-time) production system, which applies cost

FIGURE 1.16 COST UNITS

Examples of cost units

Industry sector	Cost unit
Brewing	Barrel
Brick-making	1,000 bricks
Coal mining	Tonne/ton
Electricity	Kilowatt hour (KwH)
Engineering	Contract, job
Oil	Barrel, tonne, litre
Hotel/Catering	Room/meal
Professional services	Chargeable hour, job, contract
Education	Course, enrolled student, successful student
Hospitals	Patient day

Activity	Cost unit
Credit control	Account maintained
Materials storage/handling	Requisition unit issued/received, material movement value issued/received
Personnel administration	Personnel record
Selling	Customer call, value of sales, orders taken

to the output of a process. Costs do not mirror the flow of products through the production process, but are attached to output produced (finished goods stock and cost of sales), on the assumption that such backflushed costs are a realistic measure of the actual costs incurred. *See* just-in-time (Chapter 2).

costing, life-cycle   Maintenance of physical asset cost records over entire asset lives, so that decisions concerning the acquisition use or disposal of assets can be made in a way that achieves the optimum asset usage at the lowest possible cost to the entity. The term may be applied to the profiling of cost over a product's life, including the pre-production stage (*terotechnology*), and to both company and industry life cycles. *See* Figure 1.18.

costing, standard   Control technique that reports *variances* by comparing

FIGURE 1.17 PRICING OF STOCK ISSUES

Date	Purchase quantity	Unit cost	Total cost	Issue quantity	Issue cost	Balance	
	Units	$	$	Units	$	Units	$
1 April	200	1.20	240	–	–	200	240
12 April	350	1.30	455	–	–	550	695
13 April	420	1.10	462	–	–	970	1,157
15 April	–			500	(a)	470	(b)

The valuation of the issues made on 15 April (a) and the valuation of the residual stock (b) are as follows

Valuation of issues: *Valuation of residual stock:*

FIFO: (200 × $1.20) + (300 × $1.30) = $630 $527
LIFO: (420 × $1.10) + (80 × $1.30) = $566 $591

Weighted average: (500 × $1,157/970) = $596 $561

Note: The valuation of stock issues is independent of any policy with respect to the order in which physical stock should be issued, which would, where practicable, be FIFO.

FIGURE 1.18 LIFE CYCLE COSTS OF A PRODUCT OR SERVICE

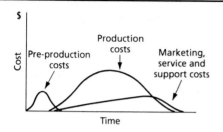

actual costs to pre-set standards so facilitating action through *management by exception*.

customer profitability analysis (CPA)
Analysis of the revenue streams and service costs associated with specific customers or customer groups.

direct product profitability (DPP) Used primarily within the retail sector, DPP involves the attribution of both the purchase price and other indirect costs (for example distribution, warehousing and retailing) to each product line. Thus a net profit, as opposed to a gross profit, can be identified for each product. The cost attribution process utilises a variety of measures (for example warehousing space and transport time) to reflect the resource consumption of individual products.

environmental management accounting
Identification, collection, analysis and use of two types of information for internal decision making: physical information on the use, flows and rates of energy, water and materials (including wastes); and monetary information on environment-related costs, earnings and savings (EMARIC).

equivalent units Notional whole units representing uncompleted work. Used to apportion costs between work in progress and completed output, and in performance assessment.

feasible region Area contained within all of the constraint lines shown on a graphical depiction of a linear programming problem. All feasible combinations of output are contained within or located on the boundaries of the feasible region. *See* Figure 1.19.

first in, first out (FIFO) *See* stock (inventory) valuation.

gross profit percentage *See* ratio, gross profit to sales revenue.

high/low method Method of estimating cost behaviour by comparing the total costs associated with two different levels of output. The difference in costs is assumed to be caused by variable costs increasing, allowing unit variable cost to be calculated. Following from this, since total cost is known, the fixed cost can be derived.

incremental analysis Analysis of changes in costs and revenues caused by a change in activity. A significant change may cause changes to variable and fixed costs and possibly to selling prices. Incremental or differential costs and revenues are compared to determine the financial effect of the change.

job Customer order or task of relatively short duration.

FIGURE 1.19 FEASIBLE REGION

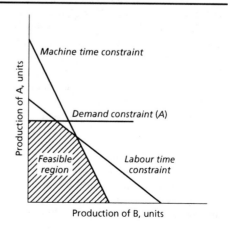

job cost sheet   Detailed record of the amount, and cost, of the labour, material and overhead charged to a specific job.

joint products   Two or more products produced by the same process and separated in processing, each having a sufficiently high saleable value to merit recognition as a main product. *See* by-product.

key performance indicators (KPIs)
Quantitative but not necessarily financial metrics that can indicate progress or lack of progress towards a strategic objective. For example, metrics may be devised for safety, quality, turnover of key staff. Key performance indicators were important to the idea of *management by objectives* and are integral to the *scorecard* ideas developed in the 1990s.

knowledge management   Systematic process of finding, selecting, organising, distilling and presenting information so as to improve comprehension of a specific area of interest. Specific activities help focus the organisation on acquiring, storing and utilising knowledge for such things as problem solving, dynamic learning, strategic planning and decision making.

last in, first out (LIFO)   *See* stock (inventory) valuation.

learning curve   Mathematical expression of the commonly observed effect that, as complex and labour-intensive procedures are repeated, unit labour times tend to decrease. The equation (*see* Figure 1.20) usually relates the average time taken per unit/batch to the cumulative number of units/batches produced. An alternative, little used, formulation uses the same equation but relates the incremental (not average) time for the nth unit to the cumulative number of units/batches produced.

management accounting   Management accounting is the application of the principles of accounting and financial management to create, protect, preserve and increase value for the stakeholders of

for-profit and not-for-profit enterprises in the public and private sectors.

Management accounting is an integral part of management. It requires the identification, generation, presentation, interpretation and use of relevant information to:
- Inform strategic decisions and formulate business strategy
- Plan long, medium and short-run operations
- Determine capital structure and fund that structure
- Design reward strategies for executives and shareholders
- Inform operational decisions
- Control operations and ensure the efficient use of resources
- Measure and report financial and non-financial performance to management and other stakeholders
- Safeguard tangible and intangible assets
- Implement corporate governance procedures, risk management and internal controls.

management by exception   Practice of concentrating on activities that require attention and ignoring those which appear to be conforming to expectations.

Typically, standard cost variances or variances from budget are used to identify those activities that require attention.

margin   Difference between the selling price and cost of sales expressed either as a percentage of sales or as an absolute amount. *See* mark-up.

marginal revenue   Additional revenue generated from the sale of one additional unit of output.

maximax criterion   Criterion used to make a choice between alternative strategies. This favours the strategy that might lead to the highest possible profit, irrespective of the probability of that profit actually being achieved and the outcome if it is not successful.

FIGURE 1.20 LEARNING CURVE

Example:

A team of technicians has assembled the first of a new model of aircraft engine in a total of 2,000 hours. Assuming an 80% learning curve, determine:

1. How long it will take to manufacture the next engine
2. How long it will take to manufacture the next three engines
3. Having already produced two engines, the average time per engine required for the next six

Engines	Cumulative engines	Average hours per engine	Cumulative hours
1	1	2,000	2,000
1	2	1,600 (2,000 × 0.8)	3,200
2	4	1,280 (1,600 × 0.8)	5,120
4	8	1,024 (1,280 × 0.8)	8,192

1. The next engine will take (3,200 − 2,000) hours = 1,200 hours
2. The next three engines will take (5,120 − 2,000) hours = 3,120 hours
3. (8,192 − 3,200)/6 = 832 hours

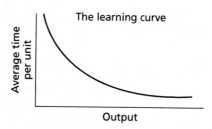

The learning curve can also be expressed mathematically as:

$$Y = ax^\beta$$

Where Y is the average time taken per unit/batch to produce a cumulative number of units/batches:
    a is the time required to produce the first unit
    x is the cumulative number of units to be produced
    β is the coefficient of learning, which can be calculated as:

$$\frac{\text{logarithm of rate of learning*}}{\text{logarithm of 2.0}}$$

* for an 80% learning curve, this would be log 0.8

maximin criterion   Criterion used to make a choice between alternative strategies. This favours the strategy that generates the highest profit if the worst outcome occurs.

minimax regret criterion   Criterion used to make a choice between alternative strategies. This is the difference between the best and worst possible payoff for each option. This criterion favours the strategy that minimises the maximum regret.

noise   Random fluctuations that can be mistaken for important information. Noise can confuse or divert attention from relevant information; efficiency in a system is enhanced as the ratio of information to noise increases.

non-financial performance measures Measures of performance based on non-financial information that may originate in and be used by operating departments to monitor and control their activities without any accounting input.

Non-financial performance measures may give a more timely indication of the levels of performance achieved than financial measures do, and may be less susceptible to distortion by factors such as uncontrollable variations in the effect of market forces on operations.

Non-financial measures are now integrated with financial measures in systems such as the balanced scorecard™. Examples of non-financial performance measures:

Area assessed	Performance measure
Service quality	Number of complaints
	Proportion of repeat
	bookings
	Customer waiting time
	On-time deliveries
Production performance	Set-up times
	Number of suppliers
	Days' inventory in
	hand
	Output per employee
	Material yield percentage
	Schedule adherence
	Proportion of output
	requiring rework
	Manufacturing lead
	times
Marketing effectiveness	Trend in market share
	Sales volume growth
	Customer visits per
	salesperson
	Client contact hours per
	salesperson
	Sales volume forecast v.
	actual
	Number of customers
	Customer survey
	response information
Personnel	Number of complaints
	received
	Staff turnover
	Days lost through
	absenteeism
	Days lost through
	accidents/sickness
	Training time per
	employee

The values expected may vary significantly between industries/sectors.

normal loss   Expected loss, allowed for in the budget, and normally calculated as a percentage of the good output from a process during a period of time. Normal losses are generally either valued at zero or at their disposal values.

operational gearing   Relationship of fixed cost to total cost of an operating unit. The greater the proportion of total costs that are fixed (high operational gearing), the greater is the advantage to the organisation of increasing sales volume. Conversely, should sales volumes drop, a highly geared organisation would find the high proportion of fixed costs to be a major problem, possibly causing a rapid swing from profitability into loss. Gearing may also be referred to as leverage. *See* ratio, gearing/leverage.

overhead absorption rate   A means of attributing overhead to a product or service, based for example on direct labour hours, direct labour cost or machine hours.
direct labour cost percentage rate   Overhead absorption rate based on direct labour cost.
direct labour hour rate   Overhead absorption rate based on direct labour hours.
machine hour rate   Overhead absorption rate based on machine hours. *See* Figure 1.1.

payroll analysis   Analysis of labour costs for accounting purposes identifying, for example: gross pay by department, operation or product; and/or gross pay analysed into direct pay or lost time.

performance measurement   Process of assessing the proficiency with which a reporting entity succeeds, by the economic acquisition of resources and their efficient and effective deployment, in achieving its objectives. Performance measures may be based on non-financial as well as on financial information. *See* non-financial performance measures.

profit margin

(sales − cost of sales)

This can be expressed either as a value or as a percentage of sales value. The profit margin may be calculated at different stages, hence the terms *gross* and *net profit margin*.

The level of profit reported is also influenced by the extent of the application of accounting conventions, and by the method of product costing used, for example marginal or absorption costing.

profit–volume/contribution graph   Graph showing the effect on contribution and on overall profit of changes in sales volume or value. *See* Figure 1.6.

profitability index

$$\frac{\text{Present value of cash inflows}}{\text{Initial investment}}$$

Used in investment appraisal. Represents the net present value of each $1 invested in a project.

project costing   *See* contract costing (cost accounting for cost objects).

qualitative factors   Factors that are relevant to a decision but are not expressed numerically.

quantitative factors   Factors that are relevant to a decision and are expressed numerically.

ratio, accounting rate of return

$$\frac{\text{Average annual profit from an investment} \times 100}{\text{Average investment}}$$

Sometimes used in investment appraisal, derived in the same way as return on investment. Unlike net present value and internal rate of return, the ratio is based on profits not cash flows. Exclusive use of this ratio is not recommended.

ratio, asset cover

$$\frac{\text{Net tangible assets before deducting overdraft and other borrowings}}{\text{Total borrowings including overdraft}}$$

Indicates the safety of lenders' money. Net tangible assets are usually calculated after deducting trade payables (hence, net).

ratio, asset value per share

$$\frac{\text{Total assets} - \text{liabilities}}{\text{Number of issued equity shares}}$$

Shows the value of net assets per share and may aid investment and disinvestment decisions. Note that this ratio is equivalent to *net worth per share*.

ratio, bad debts

$$\frac{\text{Bad debts} \times 100}{\text{Revenue on credit}}$$

Numerator and denominator should relate to the same period, bad debts should be calculated as an average figure for the relevant time period.

$$\frac{\text{Bad debts} \times 100}{\text{Total receivables at a point in time}}$$

Indicates the significance of bad debts as a proportion of debtors.

ratio, capacity   Capacity is usually measured in standard units, typically standard labour or machine hours in manufacturing, and, correspondingly, standard hours in professional practices such as accountants and consultants. The more commonly used capacity levels are:

full capacity   Output achievable if sales orders, supplies, workforce, for example, were all available.

practical capacity   Full capacity less an allowance for known, unavoidable volume losses.

budgeted capacity   Standard hours planned for the budget period, taking account of, for example, budgeted sales, workforce and expected efficiency.

normal capacity   Measure of the long-run average level of capacity that may be expected. This is often used in setting the budgeted fixed overhead absorption rate (giving it stability over time, although budgeted fixed overhead volume variances may be produced as a consequence).

On the following given data, the related ratios are set out below:

Full capacity standard hours	100
Practical capacity standard hours	95
Budgeted capacity (budgeted input hours, 90 at 90% efficiency)	81
Actual input hours	85
Standard hours produced	68

idle capacity ratio

$$\frac{(\text{Practical capacity} - \text{budgeted capacity}) \times 100}{\text{Practical capacity}}$$

$$= \frac{(95 - 81) \times 100}{95} = 15\%$$

Indicates the budgeted shortfall in capacity as a proportion of practical capacity.

production volume ratio

$$\frac{\text{Standard hours produced} \times 100}{\text{Budgeted capacity}}$$

$$= \frac{68 \times 100}{81} = 84\%$$

Shows the actual output as a proportion of budgeted output.

production efficiency ratio

$$\frac{\text{Standard hours produced} \times 100}{\text{Actual hours}}$$

$$= \frac{68 \times 100}{85} = 80\%$$

Measures the relationship between output produced and productive time taken, which may be measured in either direct labour or machine hours, as appropriate.

ratio, capital turnover

$$\frac{\text{Revenue for the year}}{\text{Average capital employed in year}}$$

Expresses the number of times that capital is covered by sales in a year or the revenue generated by each $1 of capital employed. Capital employed is usually calculated as either:

(a) total net assets
(fixed assets + current assets – current liabilities) or
(b) capital employed
(equity + long-term debt).
The two methods are equivalent.

ratio, contribution per unit of limiting factor

$$\frac{\text{Product/service contribution}}{\text{Product/service usage of units of limiting factor}}$$

Used in short-term decision making to measure the contribution to fixed overhead and profit generated by the use of each unit of limiting factor. This is used to rank alternative uses of the limiting factor.

ratio, contribution to sales

$$\frac{(\text{Revenue} - \text{all variable costs}) \times 100}{\text{Revenue}}$$

Of particular use in product profit planning and as a means of ranking alternative products. Also important in breakeven problems that assume a constant product mix. Note, although contribution to sales ratio can be used to rank products, it cannot be used to solve limiting factor problems (unless the limiting factor is sales revenue).

ratio, creditor days   *See* ratio, payables days.

ratio, debtor days   *See* ratio, receivables days.

ratio, dividend cover

$$\frac{\text{Earnings per share}}{\text{Dividend per share}}$$

Indicates the number of times the profits attributable to the equity shareholders cover the net dividends payable for the period.

ratio, dividend payout

$$\frac{\text{Ordinary dividends for the year}}{\text{Earnings attributable to the ordinary shareholders}}$$

Shows the proportion of earnings distributed to ordinary shareholders as dividends. Indicates how safe the dividend is (as does the *dividend cover ratio*).

ratio, fixed asset turnover

$$\frac{\text{Revenue for the year}}{\text{Average net book value of fixed assets}}$$

Indicates the revenue generated by each \$1 of fixed assets, or the number of times fixed assets are turned over in the year.

ratio, gearing/leverage

Relates to financial gearing, which is the relationship between an entity's borrowings, which includes both prior charge capital, for example preference shares, and long-term debt, and its share-holders' funds (ordinary share capital plus reserves). Gearing calculations can be made in a number of ways, and may be based on capital values or on earnings/interest relationships. Overdrafts and interest paid thereon may also be included.

$$\frac{\text{Profit before interest and tax}}{\text{Profit before tax}}$$

Shows the effect of interest on the operating profit (income gearing). *See* also ratio, interest cover.

$$\frac{\text{Total long-term debt}}{\text{Shareholders' funds} + \text{long-term debt}}$$

Shows the proportion of long-term financing which is being supplied by debt (balance sheet gearing).

$$\frac{\text{Total long-term debt}}{\text{Total assets}}$$

A measure of the capacity to redeem debt obligations by the sale of assets.

$$\frac{\text{Operating cashflows} - \text{taxation paid} - \text{returns on investment and servicing of finance}}{\text{Repayments of debt due within one year}}$$

Measures ability to redeem debt. An entity with a high proportion of prior charge capital to shareholders' funds is high geared, and is low geared if the reverse situation applies.

ratio, gross profit to sales revenue (gross profit margin %)

$$\frac{(\text{Sales} - \text{cost of sales}) \times 100}{\text{Sales for the period}}$$

Used to gain an insight into the relationship between production/purchasing costs and sales revenues.

ratio, interest cover

$$\frac{\text{Profit before interest and tax}}{\text{Interest payable}}$$

Used by lenders to determine vulnerability of interest payments to a drop in profit.

ratio(s), inventory days

number of days' inventory

$$\frac{\text{Stock value}}{\text{Average daily cost of sales in period}}$$

Number of days' inventory at the forecast or recent usage rate. Can be applied to finished goods, raw material and work in progress by using appropriate numerators and denominators.

number of weeks' inventory

The efficiency of inventory utilisation is indicated by:

$$\frac{\text{Finished goods stock}}{\text{Average weekly despatches}}$$

$$\frac{\text{Raw material stock}}{\text{Average weekly raw material usage}}$$

$$\frac{\text{Work in progress}}{\text{Average weekly production}}$$

These ratios are normally calculated using appropriate values although, in certain circumstances, quantities may be used.

ratio, length of order book

$$\frac{\text{Sales value of orders outstanding}}{\text{Sales value of production per day/week/month}}$$

The sales value of production may be based on planned, current or available capacity production.

ratio(s), liquidity   Relate to working capital and indicate the ability to meet liabilities from assets available. The most commonly used are:

acid test/quick ratio

$$\frac{\text{Current assets – stock at end of period}}{\text{Current liabilities at end of period}}$$

Indicates the ability to pay creditors in the short term.

current ratio

$$\frac{\text{Current assets at end of period}}{\text{Current liabilities at end of period}}$$

An overall measure of liquidity.

ratio, margin of safety

$$\frac{(\text{Forecast revenue } - \text{ breakeven revenue}) \times 100}{\text{Forecast revenue}}$$

Indicates the percentage by which forecast revenue exceeds or falls short of that required to break even.

ratio, net profit to sales revenue (net profit margin %)

$$\frac{\text{Net profit before interest and tax} \times 100}{\text{Revenue}}$$

A key profitability ratio. If the numerator is not multiplied by 100 it shows the profit generated by each $1 of sales.

ratio, payables days

$$\frac{\text{Average trade payables}}{\text{Average daily purchases on credit terms}}$$

Indicates the average time taken, in calendar days, to pay for supplies received on credit. Adjustment is needed if the ratio is materially distorted by value added or other taxes.

ratio, price/earnings (P/E ratio)

$$\frac{\text{Market price per share}}{\text{Earnings per share}}$$

Shows the number of years it would take to recoup an equity investment from its share of the attributable profit. The P/E ratio values the shares of the company as a multiple of current or prospective earnings. The P/E ratio is the most common way of reporting the relationship between earnings and share prices, although its inverse, the earnings yield, is probably intuitively easier to grasp. A low P/E ratio implies a high earnings yield. A low P/E ratio might indicate that the market perceives earnings to be "low quality".

ratio, profit per employee

$$\frac{\text{Profit for the year before interest and tax}}{\text{Average number of employees}}$$

Indication of the effectiveness of the employment of staff. When there are full- and part-time employees, full-time equivalents should be used. *See* sales per employee.

ratio pyramid   The analysis of a primary ratio into mathematically linked secondary ratios. For example:

primary ratio

(a) $\dfrac{\text{Profit}}{\text{Capital employed}}$

Secondary ratio

(b) $\dfrac{\text{Profit}}{\text{Turnover}}$ (c) $\dfrac{\text{Turnover}}{\text{Capital employed}}$

Ratio $a = b \times c$. Ratios b and c can be analysed by further ratios if desired. The pyramid continues with further analysis of the secondary ratios. *See* Figures 1.21, 1.22 and 1.23.

ratio, receivables days

$$\frac{\text{Average trade receivables}}{\text{Average daily revenue on credit terms}}$$

Indicates the average time taken, in calendar days, to receive payment from credit customers. Adjustment is needed if the ratio is materially distorted by value added or other taxes.

ratio, sales per employee

$$\frac{\text{Revenue for the year}}{\text{Average number of employees}}$$

Indicator of labour productivity. *See* profit per employee.

FIGURE 1.21 RATIO PYRAMID FOR A MANUFACTURER

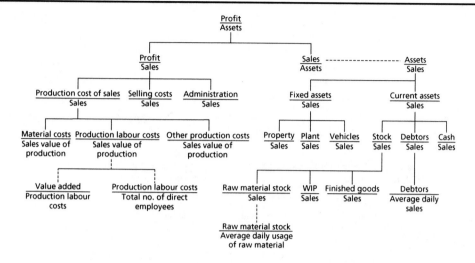

ratio, stock turnover   *See* ratio, inventory days.

reciprocal cost allocation   Method of reallocating (strictly apportioning) service centre costs in a number of iterations until all service costs have been recharged to user centres. Can also be formulated as a set of equations and solved by matrix algebra. *See* re-apportion (apportioning).

recovery   *See* overhead absorption rate.

rejects/defects   Units of output which fail a set quality standard and are subsequently rectified, sold as substandard or disposed of as scrap.

relevant costs/revenues   Costs and revenues appropriate to a specific management decision.

These are represented by future cash flows whose magnitude will vary depending upon the outcome of the management decision made. If stock is used, the relevant

FIGURE 1.22 RATIO PYRAMID FOR A RETAILER

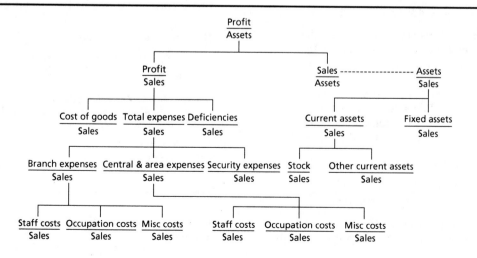

FIGURE 1.23 RATIO PYRAMID FOR SERVICES

cost, used in the determination of the profitability of the transaction, would be the cost of replacing the stock, not its original purchase price, which is a sunk cost.

Abandonment analysis, based on relevant cost and revenues, is the process of determining whether or not it is more profitable to discontinue a product or service than to continue it.

relevant range Activity levels within which assumptions about cost behaviour in breakeven analysis remain valid.

replacement price Price at which identical goods or capital equipment could be purchased at the date of valuation.

residual income Profit minus a charge for capital employed in the period. The calculation is exactly the same as that for *economic value added*.

However, in the latter case, accounting profit is often adjusted before the calculation of economic value added. *See* economic value added (Chapter 4).

return on capital employed (ROCE)

$$\frac{\text{Profit before interest and tax} \times 100}{\text{Average capital employed}}$$

Indicates the productivity of capital employed. The denominator is normally

calculated as the average of the capital employed at the beginning and the end of the year. Problems of seasonality, new capital introduced or other factors may necessitate taking the average of a number of periods within the year. The ROCE is known as the primary ratio in a ratio pyramid. *See* capital employed.

return on equity

$$\frac{\text{Profit after interest and tax}}{\text{Ordinary share capital} + \text{reserves}}$$

Form of return on capital employed which measures the return to the owners on their investment in an entity.

return on investment (ROI)

$$\frac{\text{Profit before interest and tax}}{\text{Average capital employed}}$$

Often used to assess managers' performance. Managers are responsible for all assets (normally defined as non-current assets plus net current assets). *See* ratio, capital turnover.

return on sales *See* profit margin.

scrap Discarded material having some value.

standard Benchmark measurement of resource usage or revenue or profit generation, set in defined conditions. Standards can be set on a number of bases:

(a) on an *ex ante* estimate of expected performance;
(b) on an *ex post* estimate of attainable performance;
(c) on a prior period level of performance by the same organisation;
(d) on the level of performance achieved by comparable organisations; or
(e) on the level of performance required to meet organisational objectives.

Standards may also be set at attainable levels that assume efficient levels of operation, but that include allowance for normal loss, waste and machine down time, or at ideal levels that make no allowance for the above losses, and are only attainable under the most favourable conditions. The effect of different levels on staff motivation will be an important influence on the type of standards that are used. *See* standard, *ex ante*, and standard, *ex post*.

standard cost card/standard product specification Document or digital record detailing for each individual product, the standard inputs required for production as well as the standard selling price. Inputs are normally divided into labour, material and overhead categories, and both price and quantity information is shown for each.

standard direct labour cost Planned cost of direct labour.

(standard direct labour time for one unit of product × standard labour rate)

There are separate calculations for different processes and/or grades of labour.

standard, *ex ante* Before the event. An *ex ante* budget or standard is set before a period of activity commences.

standard, *ex post* After the event. An *ex post* budget, or standard, is set after the end of a period of activity, when it can represent the optimum achievable level of performance in the conditions which were experienced. Thus the budget can be flexed, and standards can reflect factors such as unanticipated changes in technology and in price levels. This approach may be used in conjunction with sophisticated cost and revenue modelling to determine how far both the plan and the achieved results differed from the performance that would have been expected in the circumstances which were experienced.

standard hour or minute Amount of work achievable, at standard efficiency levels, in an hour or minute.

standard performance – labour Level of efficiency which appropriately trained, motivated and resourced employees can achieve in the long-run.

stock (inventory) valuation

average cost Used to price issues of goods or materials at the weighted average cost of all units held.

first-in, first-out (FIFO) Used to price issues of goods or materials based on the cost of the oldest units held, irrespective of the sequence in which the actual issue of units held takes place. Closing stock is, therefore, valued at the cost of the oldest purchases.

last-in, first-out (LIFO) Used to price issues of goods or materials based on the cost of the most recently received units. Cost of sales in the income statement is, therefore, valued at the cost of the most recent purchases. LIFO is permitted under US GAAP but is not permitted by IAS 2 (or SSAP 9 in the UK).

standard cost All units held as stock are valued at a standard cost so that units issued and closing stock are valued at standard cost, with any variance between actual costs incurred and standard cost reported in the income statement in the period in which it is incurred. All the above methods value stock at cost, but IAS 2 requires all stocks to be valued at the lower of cost and net realisable value. *See* fair value less costs to sell (Chapter 3).

strategic business unit Section, usually a division, within a larger organisation that has a significant degree of autonomy, typically being responsible for developing and marketing its own products and services.

super variable costing   *See* throughput accounting.

theory, agency   Hypothesis that attempts to explain elements of organisational behaviour through an understanding of the relationships between principals (such as shareholders) and agents (such as entity managers and accountants). A conflict may exist between the actions undertaken by agents in furtherance of their own self-interest, and those required to promote the interests of the principals. Within the hierarchy of entities, the same goal incongruence may arise when divisional managers promote their own self-interest over those of other divisions and of the entity generally.

theory, contingency   Theory relating to the design of accounting systems that presupposes that systems can be effectively designed to suit the circumstances of the firm including its technology, entity structure and its competitive environment. For example, it is argued that mechanistic (hierarchical, bureaucratic) systems can be effective in stable environments. Organic (typically flatter, task-related) systems are said to be more appropriate in more turbulent, competitive environments.

theory of constraints (TOC)   Procedure based on identifying bottlenecks (constraints), maximising their use, subordinating other facilities to the demands of the bottleneck facilities, alleviating bottlenecks and re-evaluating the whole system. (Goldratt created this concept).

throughput   Term defined, in work by Goldratt, as sales minus material and component costs. Similar to contribution except material is considered the only variable cost. Goldratt argues that labour costs should be treated as fixed. In Goldratt's analysis *operating expense* is all non-material costs and *inventory cost* is defined as the cost of assets employed.

throughput accounting (TA)   Variable cost accounting presentation based on the definition of throughput (sales minus material and component costs). Sometimes referred to as *super variable costing* because only material costs are treated as variable.

throughput per bottleneck minute   Method of ranking products that share the same (bottleneck) facility. Very similar to the use of contribution per unit of limiting factor.

throughput ratios   Several ratios were defined by Galloway and Waldron based on the definition of throughput. The TA (throughput accounting) ratio is:

$$\frac{\text{Throughput per bottleneck minute}}{\text{Factory cost per bottleneck minute}}$$

Note: Galloway and Waldron define factory cost in the same way that Goldratt defines operating expense. *See* throughput.

If the TA ratio is greater than 1 the product in question is "profitable" because, if all capacity were devoted to that product, the throughput generated would exceed the total factory cost. If there was a bottleneck products could be ranked by a variant of the TA ratio (although the ranking is the same as that derived by the use of throughput per bottleneck minute). Other performance ratios suggested include:

$$\frac{\text{throughput}}{\text{labour cost}}$$

and

$$\frac{\text{throughput}}{\text{material cost}}$$

transfer price   Price at which goods or services are transferred between different units in the same company. May be set on a number of bases, such as marginal cost, full cost, market price or negotiation. For the transfer of goods between units in different countries, tax implications mean that the respective governments have to accept the method used. They are likely to insist on *arm's-length transfer prices*.

uniform accounting   System by which different entities in the same industry adopt common concepts, principles and assumptions in order to generate accounting information that facilitates inter-entity comparison or a system of classifying financial accounts in a similar manner within defined business sectors of a national economy to ensure comparability.

value added Traditionally the difference between sales revenue and the cost of materials and bought-out services. Alternatively, it might be calculated as the sum of profit, interest and all conversion costs. Recently, more commonly used in the context of *economic value added*. *See* economic value added, Chapter 4.

value analysis Systematic interdisciplinary examination of factors affecting the cost of a product or service, in order to devise means of achieving the specified purpose most economically at the required standard of quality and reliability (BS 3138)[1].

value driver Activity or organisational focus which enhances the perceived value of a product or service in the perception of the consumer, and which therefore creates value for the producer. Advanced technology, reliability or reputation for customer care may be value drivers.

value engineering Redesign of an activity, product or service so that value to the customer is enhanced while costs are reduced (or, at least, increase by less than the resulting price increase).

variance Difference between a planned, budgeted or standard cost and the actual cost incurred. The same comparisons may be made for revenues.

variance, administrative cost Measurement of the extent of any over- or underspend on administrative costs.
(budgeted cost of administration − actual cost)

variance analysis Evaluation of performance by means of variances, whose timely reporting should maximise the opportunity for managerial action. *See* Figure 1.34.

[1] Permission to reproduce extracts from BS 3138: 1992 is granted by BSI. British Standards can be obtained from BSI Customer Services, 389 Chiswich High Road, London W4 4AL. email: cservices@bsi_global.com.

variance, budget Difference, for each cost or revenue element in a budget, between the budgeted amount and the actual cost or revenue. Where flexible budgeting is employed, it is the difference between the flexed budget and the actual value.

variance, direct labour efficiency Standard labour cost of any change from the standard level of labour efficiency.
((actual production in standard hours − actual hours worked) × standard direct labour rate per hour)
See Figure 1.28.

variance, direct labour idle time This variance occurs when the hours paid exceed the hours worked and there is an extra cost caused by this idle time. Its computation increases the accuracy of the labour efficiency variance.
((hours paid − hours worked) × standard direct labour rate per hour)

variance, direct labour mix Subdivision of the direct labour efficiency variance. If grades of labour can be substituted the mix variance measures the cost of any variation from the standard mix of grades.
((actual hours for grade − hours for grade based on total labour hours split in standard proportions) × (weighted average cost per hour − standard cost per hour))
Alternatively, the calculation can be made without reference to the relative cost of the various labour inputs.
((hours for grade based on total labour hours split in standard proportions − actual labour hours for grade) × standard cost per hour)
When the individual grade variances are summed the same total mix variance is calculated. The first method is recommended because the individual grade variances are meaningful, whereas in the second method they are not.

variance, direct labour rate Indicates the actual cost of any change from the standard labour rate of remuneration.
((actual hours paid × standard direct labour rate per hour) − (actual hours paid × actual direct labour rate per hour))
See Figure 1.28.

variance, direct labour total   Indicates the difference between the standard direct labour cost of the output which has been produced and the actual direct labour cost incurred.

   ((standard hours produced × standard direct labour rate per hour) – (actual hours paid × actual direct labour rate per hour))
See Figure 1.28.

variance, direct labour yield   Subdivision of the direct labour efficiency variance. Measures the effect on cost of any difference between the actual usage of labour and that justified by the output produced. It is recommended that the variance be calculated in total and not for individual labour grade inputs.

   ((standard labour hours allowed for actual output – actual labour hours input) × standard weighted average cost per direct labour hour)

   It may also be calculated in the following way:

   ((standard labour hours required for good output – actual labour hours worked in standard proportions) × standard cost per labour hour)

variance, direct material mix   Subdivision of the material usage variance. If different materials can be substituted the mix variance measures the cost of any variation from the standard mix of materials.

   ((actual quantity of material – quantity of material based on total material quantity split in standard proportions) × (weighted average cost per kg, litre, other – standard cost per kg, litre, other))

   Alternatively, the calculation can be made without reference to the relative cost of the various material inputs.

   ((quantity of material based on total material quantity split in standard proportions – actual quantity of material) × standard cost per kg, litre, other),

   When the individual material variances are summed the same total mix variance is calculated. The first method is recommended because the individual material variances are meaningful, whereas in the second method they are not. *See* Figure 1.31.

variance, direct material price   Difference between the actual price paid for purchased materials and their standard cost.

   ((actual quantity of material purchased × standard price) – actual cost of material purchased)

   The material price variance may also be calculated at the time of material withdrawal from stores. In this case, the stock accounts are maintained at actual cost, price variances being extracted at the time of material usage rather than of purchase.

   ((actual material used × standard cost) – actual cost of material used)

   The latter method is not usually recommended because one of the advantages of a standard costing system is the valuation of all stock at standard costs. *See* Figure 1.28.

variance, direct material total
Measurement of the difference between the standard material cost of the output produced and the actual material cost incurred.

   (standard material cost of output produced – actual cost of material purchased)

   Where the quantities of material purchased and used are different, the total variance should be calculated as the sum of the usage and price variances.

variance, direct material usage   Measures efficiency in the use of material, by comparing standard material usage for actual production with actual material used, the difference is valued at standard cost.

   ((actual production × standard material per unit – actual material usage) × standard cost per kg, litre, other)

   The direct material usage variance may be divided into mix and yield variances if several materials are mixed in standard proportions. *See* Figure 1.28.

variance, direct material yield   Subdivision of the material usage variance. Measures the effect on cost of any difference between the actual usage of material and that justified by the output produced. It is recommended that the variance be calculated in total and not for individual material inputs.

((standard material quantity allowed for actual output – actual material quantity input) × standard weighted average cost per kg, litre, other)

It may also be calculated in the following way:

((standard material quantity required for actual output – actual material quantities used in standard proportions) × standard cost per kg, litre, other)

See Figure 1.31.

variance, fixed production overhead capacity
Little used subdivision of the fixed production overhead volume variance.

variance, fixed production overhead efficiency
Little used subdivision of the fixed production overhead volume variance.

variance, fixed production overhead expenditure
The difference between the fixed production overhead which should have been incurred in the period, and that which was incurred.

(budgeted fixed production overhead – actual fixed production overhead)

variance, fixed production overhead total
The difference between the fixed production overhead absorbed by actual production and the actual fixed production overhead incurred.

((actual production in standard hours × fixed production overhead absorption rate per hour) – actual fixed production overhead)

This variance can be divided into fixed production overhead expenditure and fixed production overhead volume variances.

variance, fixed production overhead volume
A measure of the over- or under-absorption of overhead cost caused by actual production volume differing from that budgeted.

((actual production in standard hours × fixed production overhead absorption rate per hour) – budgeted fixed production overhead)

See Figure 1.28.

variance, joint
A variance which is caused by both the prices and quantities of inputs differing from the specifications in the original standard. *See* Figure 1.24.

variance, market share
A subdivision of the sales volume contribution or margin variance, applicable when the actual market size of a product or product group is known. It indicates the change in contribution or margin caused by a change in market share.

((actual sales volume – sales volume based on budgeted share of actual market) × standard contribution or margin per unit) *See* Figure 1.33.

variance, market size
A subdivision of the sales volume contribution or margin variance, applicable when the actual market size of a product or product group is known. It indicates the change in

FIGURE 1.24 JOINT VARIANCES

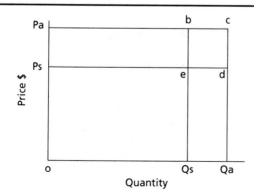

Ps is the standard material price
Pa is the actual material price paid
Qs is the standard quantity of material
Qa is the actual quantity of material used

The area of the box *bcde* represents the joint variance, whose cause lies in both the quantity and the price exceeding the standard allowances. A standard costing system normally incorporates the joint variance into the material price variance computation contribution or margin caused by a change in the size of the market.

((sales volume based on budgeted share of actual market – budgeted sales volume) × standard contribution or margin per unit) *See* Figure 1.33.

variance, marketing cost   Where marketing cost contains both fixed and variable components, separate variances should be calculated.

(budgeted marketing cost – actual marketing cost)

variance, operational   Classification of variances in which non-standard performance is defined as being that which differs from an *ex post* standard.

Operational variances can relate to any element of the standard product specification. *See* Figure 1.34.

variance, planning   Classification of variances caused by *ex ante* budget allowances being changed to an *ex post* basis. Also known as a revision variance. *See* Figure 1.34.

variance, sales mix contribution/profit margin   Subdivision of the sales volume contribution/profit margin variance. The change in the contribution/profit margin caused by a change in the mix of the products or services sold.

((actual sales units – sales units based on total sales in budget proportions) × (standard contribution/profit margin per unit – budget weighted average contribution/profit margin per unit))

This method of computation highlights the contribution/profit margin effect, by product, of sales deviating from budget proportions. A favourable variance denotes either selling proportionately more of a relatively high contribution/profit margin product or proportionately less of a relatively low contribution/profit margin product.

It can also be calculated as:

((actual sales units – sales units based on total sales in budget proportions) × standard contribution/profit margin per unit)

When summed up for all products this method gives the same result as the first method. The first method is recommended because the results for individual products are meaningful, whereas in the second method they are not. *See* Figure 1.32.

variance, sales price   Change in revenue caused by the actual selling price differing from that budgeted.

(actual sales revenue – (actual sales volume × standard selling price per unit)) *See* Figure 1.28.

variance, sales quantity contribution/profit Subdivision of the sales volume contribution/profit variance. It is relevant if there are multiple products and the actual sales mix differs from the budgeted sales mix. In these situations this variance, together with the sales mix contribution/profit variance, will comprise the sales volume contribution/profit variance (for all products). It can be calculated in either of the following ways:

((actual total sales volume – budgeted total sales volume) × budgeted weighted average contribution/profit per unit)

or

((actual total sales volume in budgeted mix – budgeted sales volume) × budgeted contribution/profit per unit)

If the second method is used the sum of the variances for all products will be the same as the result obtained using the first formula. *See* Figure 1.32.

variance, sales volume contribution/profit Measure of the effect on contribution/profit of not achieving the budgeted volume of sales.

((actual sales volume – budgeted sales volume) × standard contribution/profit per unit) *See* Figure 1.28.

variance, sales volume revenue   Change in sales revenue caused by sales volume differing from that budgeted.

((actual sales volume – budget sales) × standard selling price per unit)

This variance is logical but little used because it cannot be combined with contribution/profit variances in reconciling budget with actual contribution/profit. In principle, if several products are considered, the sales mix revenue variance and total sales volume revenue variance can be calculated. *See* variance, sales mix contribution and variance, sales quantity contribution/profit for the method of derivation – substitute "selling price" for "contribution" in the appropriate formula.

variance, total profit   Difference between the actual profit and the profit in the budget.

The total profit variance is the sum of all the subsidiary variances.

(actual profit – budgeted profit)

variance, variable production overhead efficiency   Standard variable overhead cost of any change from the standard level of efficiency.

((actual production in standard hours – actual hours worked) × standard variable overhead rate per hour)

This is directly analogous to the calculation of *direct labour efficiency variance* and implicitly assumes that variable overhead is recovered on a direct labour hour base. However, the formula can equally be used if variable overhead is recovered on a machine or process hour base. *See* Figure 1.28.

variance, variable production overhead expenditure   Indicates the actual cost of any change from the standard rate per hour.

((standard variable rate per hour – actual variable rate per hour) × actual hours worked)

Hours refer to either labour or machine hours depending on the recovery base chosen for variable production overhead. *See* Figure 1.28.

variance, variable production overhead total   Measures the difference between variable overhead that should be used for actual output and variable production overhead actually used.

((actual production in standard hours × standard variable production overhead absorption rate per hour) – actual cost incurred)

The *variable production overhead efficiency* and *rate variances* are subdivisions of this variance.

waste   Discarded material having no value.

FIGURE 1.25 CHART OF VARIANCES (MARGINAL COSTING PRINCIPLES)

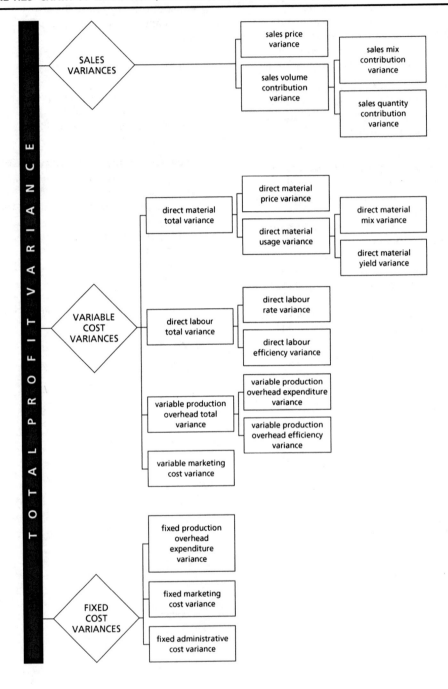

FIGURE 1.26 CHART OF VARIANCES (ABSORPTION COSTING PRINCIPLES)

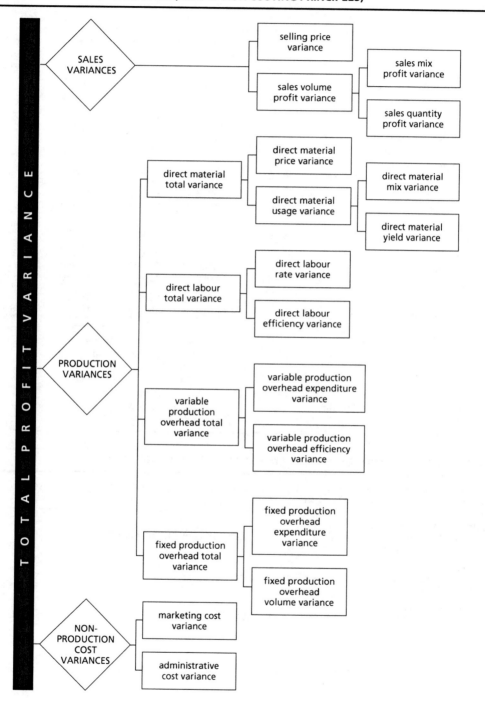

FIGURE 1.27 OPERATING STATEMENT WITH FLEXED BUDGET

Period ....

	Standard per unit	Fixed Budget*	Flexed Budget	Actual	Flexible Budget Variance
No. of units made and sold	1	1,000	1,100	1,100	
	$	$	$	$	$
Sales	70.00	70,000	77,000	82,500	5,500
Direct material 1 kg @ $15	15.00	15,000	16,500	17,000	(500)
Direct labour 1 hr @ $10	10.00	10,000	11,000	11,250	(250)
Variable production overhead: 1 hr @ $2.50	2.50	2,500	2,750	3,050	(300)
Total variable costs	27.50	27,500	30,250	31,300	
Contribution	42.50	42,500	46,750	51,200	
Fixed production overhead: 1 hr @ $5	5.00	5,000	5,000	5,300	(300)
Gross profit	37.50	37,500	41,750	45,900	
Fixed marketing cost		12,500	12,500	12,950	(450)
Fixed administrative cost		13,000	13,000	13,550	(550)
		25,500	25,500	26,500	
Operating profit		12,000	16,250	19,400	3,150

$4,250
Sales volume
contribution
variance

$3,150
Price, usage and
expenditure
variances

Fixed budget profit − actual profit =

$7,400
Total profit variance

FIGURE 1.28 STANDARD COSTING VARIANCES (MARGINAL COSTING BASIS)

These calculations are based on Figure 1.27 and note that 1,200 kg of materials were purchased and used; 1,250 labour hours were worked

Sales volume contribution
(actual sales volume − budgeted sales volume) × standard contribution per unit
$(1,100 − 1,000) × 42.50 = 4,250

Sales price
actual sales revenue − (actual sales volume × standard selling price per unit)
$82,500 − (1,100 × $70)$ = 5,500

Direct material price
(Actual quantity of material purchased × standard price) − actual cost of material purchased
$(1,200 × $15) − $17,000$ = 1,000

Direct material usage
(Actual production × standard material cost per unit) − (actual material used × standard material cost per unit)
$(1,100 × $15) − (1,200 × $15)$ = (1,500)

Direct labour rate
(Actual hours paid × standard direct labour rate per hour) − (actual hours paid × actual direct labour rate per hour)
$(1,250 × $10) − $11,250$ = 1,250

FIGURE 1.28 *CONTINUED*

Direct labour efficiency
(Actual production in standard hours − actual hours worked)
× standard direct labour rate per hour
(1,100 × 1 − 1,250) × $10   = (1,500)

Variable production overhead expenditure
(standard variable rate per hour − actual variable rate per hour)
× actual hours worked
($2.50 − 3,050/1,250) × 1,250   =   75

Variable production overhead efficiency
(actual production in standard hours − actual hours worked)
× standard variable overhead rate per hour
(1,100 × 1 − 1,250) × $2.50   =   (375)

Fixed production overhead expenditure
Budgeted fixed production overhead − actual fixed production overhead
$5,000 − $5,300   =   (300)

ADDITIONAL VARIANCES FOR STANDARD ABSORPTION COSTING

Sales volume profit
(actual sales volume − budgeted sales volume) × standard profit per unit
(1,100 − 1,000) × $37.50   = 3,750

Fixed production overhead volume
(Actual production in standard hours × standard fixed production
overhead absorption rate per hour) − budgeted fixed production overhead
(1,100 × 1 × $5) − $5,000   =   500

FIGURE 1.29 OPERATING STATEMENT – STANDARD MARGINAL COSTING

Period ....

	$	$	$	$
Budgeted sales				70,000
Budgeted variable cost of sales				27,500
Budgeted contribution				42,500
Sales volume contribution variance				4,250
Budgeted contribution from actual sales				46,750
Variances		(F)	(A)	
Sales price		5,500	–	
Direct material usage		–	(1,500)	
Direct material price		1,000	–	
Direct labour efficiency		–	(1,500)	
Direct labour rate		1,250	–	
Variable overhead efficiency		–	(375)	
Variable overhead expenditure		75	–	
		7,825	(3,375)	4,450
Actual contribution				51,200
Fixed costs				

	$ Budget		$ Expenditure variance	
Production	5,000		(300)	
Marketing	12,500		(450)	
Administration	13,000		(550)	
	30,500		(1,300)	31,800
Actual profit				19,400

FIGURE 1.30 OPERATING STATEMENT – STANDARD ABSORPTION COSTING

Period ....

	$	$	$
Budgeted sales			70,000
Budgeted cost of sales			32,500
			37,500
Budgeted marketing cost		12,500	
Budgeted administration cost		13,000	25,500
Budgeted profit			12,000
Sales volume profit variance			3,750
Budgeted profit from actual sales			15,750
Variances	(F)	(A)	
Sales price	5,500	–	
Marketing cost	–	(450)	
Direct material usage	–	(1,500)	
Direct material price	1,000	–	
Direct labour efficiency	–	(1,500)	
Direct labour rate	1,250	–	
Variable overhead efficiency	–	(375)	
Variable overhead expenditure	75	–	
Fixed overhead volume	500	–	
Fixed overhead expenditure	–	(300)	
Fixed administrative cost	–	(550)	
	8,325	(4,675)	3,650
Actual profit			19,400

FIGURE 1.31 WORKED EXAMPLE OF DIRECT MATERIALS YIELD AND MIX VARIANCES

1. Initial data: Materials Y and Z are mixed in the proportions 60% and 40% respectively and a standard loss of 4.5% is set. Standard and actual costs for a period show:

	Standard			Actual		
	Quantity in mix kg	Unit cost $/kg	Total cost $	Quantity in mix kg	Unit cost $/kg	Total cost $
Material Y	30,000	3.20	96,000	24,000	3.40	81,600
Material Z	20,000	2.40	48,000	21,000	2.00	42,000
Input	50,000		144,000	45,000		123,600
4.5% loss	2,250					
Output	47,750			42,000		

2. The results of the calculations and the relationships between the variances are as follows:

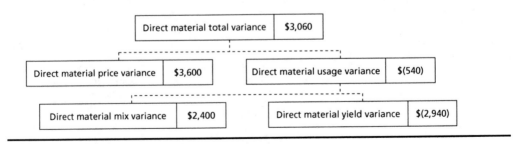

FIGURE 1.31 *CONTINUED*

	$
Direct material price variances	
(Actual quantity of material purchased × standard price) − actual cost of material purchased	
Y (24,000 × $3.20) − 81,600	= (4,800)
Z (21,000 × $2.40) − 42,000	= 8,400
	3,600

Direct material usage variances
(actual production × standard material per unit − actual material)
× standard cost per kg, litre, other
Y (((42,000 × 0.6)/0.955) − 24,000) × $3.20   = 7,640
Z (((42,000 × 0.4)/0.955) − 21,000) × $2.40   = (8,180)
  (540)

Direct material mix variance
(actual quantity of material − quantity of material based on total material
quantity split in standard proportions) × (weighted average cost per kg, litre, other
− standard cost per kg, litre, other)
Y (24,000 − 27,000) × ($2.88 − $3.20)   = 960
Z (21,000 − 18,000) × ($2.88 − $2.40)   = 1,440
  2,400

Direct material yield variance
(standard material quantity allowed for actual output − actual material
quantity input) × standard weighted average cost per kg, litre, other
(42,000/0.955 − 45,000) × $2.88   = (2,940)

Unlike mix and price variances, the yield variances for each individual
material in a mix are of no managerial interest.

Note: The material mix variance may also be calculated without reference to the relative costs of
the inputs in the mix − although the individual material mix variances then have no meaning:

(quantity of material based on total material quantity split in standard
proportions − actual quantity of material) × standard cost per kg, litre, other
Y (27,000 − 24,000) × $3.20   = 9,600
Z (18,000 − 21,000) × $2.40   = (7,200)
  2,400

FIGURE 1.32 WORKED EXAMPLE OF SALES PROFIT VARIANCES

Budgeted sales data
Product F 3,000 units with standard profit of $2.00 per unit
Product G 4,000 units with standard profit of $2.50 per unit
Product H 3,000 units with standard profit of $3.00 per unit
Weighted average standard profit is $2.50 per unit

Actual sales data
Product F 3,000 units
Product G 3,000 units
Product H 6,000 units

Sales volume profit variance $
(actual sales volume − budgeted sales volume)
× standard contribution/profit per unit
Product F (3,000 − 3,000) × $2.00   = −
Product G (3,000 − 4,000) × $2.50   = (2,500)
Product H (6,000 − 3,000) × $3.00   = 9,000
  6,500

Sales quantity profit variance
(actual total sales volume − budgeted total sales volume) × budgeted weighted average
contribution/profit per unit
(12,000 − 10,000) × $2.50   = 5,000

FIGURE 1.32 *CONTINUED*

Sales mix profit variance
(actual sales units − sales units based on total sales in budget proportions)
× (standard profit per unit − budget weighted average profit per unit)

Product F (3,000 − 3,600) × ($2.00 − $2.50)	=	300
Product G (3,000 − 4,800) × ($2.50 − $2.50)	=	−
Product H (6,000 − 3,600) × ($3.00 − $2.50)	=	1,200
		1,500

The sales mix profit variance can also be calculated as follows (but individual variances have no meaning)
(actual sales units − sales units based on total sales in budget proportions)
× standard profit per unit

Product F (3,000 − 3,600) × $2.00	=	(1,200)
Product G (3,000 − 4,800) × $2.50	=	(4,500)
Product H (6,000 − 3,600) × $3.00	=	7,200
		1,500

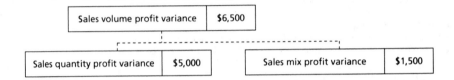

Sales volume profit variance	$6,500

Sales quantity profit variance	$5,000		Sales mix profit variance	$1,500

Note 1   Where unit quantities are not available or relevant, units would be replaced by sales, and profit per unit replaced by profit to sales ratios.

Note 2   If a marginal costing system was in operation, the following variances would be calculated with respect to sales:
 i   Sales volume contribution variance
 ii   Sales quantity contribution variance
 iii   Sales mix contribution variance
These variances would be calculated in an identical manner to the sales profit variances, although based on standard unit contribution, rather than standard unit profit.

FIGURE 1.33 WORKED EXAMPLE OF MARKET VARIANCES

These calculations are based on Figure 1.27

Budget:	1,000 units representing 20% of the market of 5,000 units
Actual:	1,100 units in a market of 6,500 units
Standard contribution:	$42.50 per unit

		$
Actual contribution	1,100 @ $42.50	46,750
Budget contribution	1,000 @ $42.50	42,500
Sales volume contribution variance		4,250
Market size variance	(6500 − 5000) × 20% × $42.50	12,750
Market share variance	(1100 − (6500 × 20%)) × $42.50	(8,500)
Sales volume contribution variance		4,250

FIGURE 1.34 WORKED EXAMPLE OF PLANNING AND OPERATIONAL VARIANCES

Before the start of the period
- the standard purchase price of material was set at $2.00 per kg

During the period
- the standard quantity of material for the output in the period: 20,000 kg
- the actual material purchased and used: 21,000 kg
- the actual purchase price paid: $2.80, due to an unforeseen occurrence which led to a material shortage

At the period end a price of $3.00 was agreed to have been an efficient buying price in the period.
The standard costing system shows an adverse direct material total variance of $18,800 made up of:
  material usage variance ($2,000)
  material price variance ($16,800)

Management wishes to distinguish between controllable and uncontrollable effects on performance.

Variance calculations
Planning price variance
  Standard material quantity × (*ex post* efficient standard
purchase price per kg − budgeted standard purchase price per kg)
  20,000 × ($3.00 − $2.00)   (20,000)
Operational usage variance
  (Actual production × *ex post* efficient standard material cost/unit) −
(actual material used × *ex post* efficient standard material cost per unit)
  (20,000 × $3.00) − (21,000 × $3.00)   ($3,000)
Operational price variance
  Actual material purchase quantity × (*ex post* efficient standard
purchase price per kg − actual purchase price per kg)
  21,000 × ($3.00 − $2.80) $4,200

Operating statement	$	$
MATERIAL		
Standard cost of output (20,000 kg × $2)		40,000
Planning price variance (20,000 kg × $1)		(20,000)
Revised standard cost of output		60,000
Operational usage variance (1,000 kg × $3)	(3,000)	
Operational price variance (21,000 kg × $0.20)	4,200	1,200
Actual cost of material used		58,800

- The planning price variance indicates that the original standard purchase price was not achievable.
- The operational usage variance indicates the standard cost (*ex post*) of the excess usage of material which took place in the period.
- The operational price variance indicates the cost saving which has been achieved by purchasing material at a price lower than the *ex post* standard.

FIGURE 1.35 PERFORMANCE MEASUREMENT RATIOS*

Asset cover and liquidity ratios indicate ability to repay borrowings

Asset cover

$$\frac{\text{Net tangible assets}}{\text{Total borrowings}}$$

$$\frac{3,119 - 356 - 288 + 1,948}{1,660 + 1,137} = 1.58$$

Note that intangible assets and goodwill are excluded from the numerator

Current ratio

$$\frac{\text{Current assets}}{\text{Current liabilities}}$$

$$\frac{1,948}{1,137} = 1.71$$

Sometimes 2:1 is considered "safe" but this depends on the industry

Acid test ratio

$$\frac{\text{Current assets} - \text{inventory}}{\text{Current liabilities}}$$

$$\frac{1,948 - 636}{1,137} = 1.15$$

Sometimes 1:1 is considered "safe" but this depends on the industry

Gearing ratios indicate the safety of debt holders' funds and ability to service debt

Balance sheet gearing

$$\frac{\text{Long-term debt}}{\text{Shareholders' funds} + \text{Long-term debt}}$$

$$\frac{1,660}{2,270 + 1,660} = 0.42$$

Note: "short-term" borrowings and the current portion of long-term borrowings might be added to the numerator if these are judged to be "really" long-term liabilities

Interest cover

$$\frac{\text{Profit before finance costs and tax}}{\text{Finance costs}}$$

$$\frac{403 + 85}{85} = 5.74$$

Indicates ability to service (rather than repay) the debt

Note: the reference to finance costs rather than interest is consistent with IAS presentation

Asset utilisation ratios indicate the efficiency with which assets are employed

(Note that, ideally, the numerators in these ratios would be *average* figures over the appropriate period. Only end of period information is available.)

Inventory days (Often calculated as the inverse: inventory turnover)

$$\frac{\text{Inventory value}}{\text{Daily cost of sales}}$$

$$\frac{636}{3,649/365} = 65 \text{ days}$$

Ideally the numerator would be average inventory over the period and there would be separate calculations with appropriate denominators for raw material inventory and finished goods inventory but this information is not available

Receivables days

$$\frac{\text{Average trade receivables}}{\text{Daily revenue on credit}}$$

$$\frac{917}{4,347/365} = 77 \text{ days}$$

If payment terms are strictly 30 days then this ratio ought to be close to 30 days, if payment terms are net 30 days then close to 45 days might be expected

*These calculations are based on Figures 3.2 and 3.6. *See* Chapter 3.

FIGURE 1.35 *CONTINUED*

| Payables days | $$\dfrac{\text{Average trade payables}}{\text{Daily purchase on credit}}$$ $$\dfrac{477}{2{,}220/365} = 78.4 \text{ days}$$ | Ideally purchases would be entered in the denominator but the most appropriate figure available is raw materials and consumables used. |

Profitability ratios indicate the profitability of sales

| Net profit margin % | $$\dfrac{\text{Profit from operation} \times 100}{\text{Revenue}}$$ $$\dfrac{285 \times 100}{4{,}347} = 6.6\%$$ | Note that profit should be related to the sales that have generated the profit. If sales relate to operations then so should profit. |
| Gross profit margin % | $$\dfrac{\text{Gross profit} \times 100}{\text{Revenue}}$$ $$\dfrac{698 \times 100}{4{,}347} = 16.1\%$$ | Useful for comparison to other entities. Gross profit % will usually be lower in retailing and wholesaling than in manufacture. |

Return on capital employed relates profitability to assets employed

Return on capital employed (ROCE)	$$\dfrac{\text{Profit before finance costs and tax}}{\text{Capital employed}}$$ $$\dfrac{403 + 85}{2{,}270 + 1{,}660} = 12.4\%$$	Often calculated to evaluate senior management performance. They have responsibility for all the capital employed (equity and debt). There is a strong argument for including all interest bearing debt in the denominator (including short-term borrowings) but these are often omitted.
Return on investment (ROI)	$$\dfrac{\text{Profit before finance costs and tax}}{\text{Investment}}$$ $$\dfrac{403 + 85}{3{,}119 + 1{,}948 - 1{,}137} = 12.4\%$$	An alternative calculation based on the use of funds (rather than there source). Again there is a strong argument that interest bearing debt, even though a "current" liability, should not be deducted in the denominator.
Return on equity	$$\dfrac{\text{Profit after finance cost}}{\text{Total equity}}$$ $$\dfrac{403}{2{,}270} = 17.8\%$$	The return to equity holders matches their return to their investment. Note the importance of matching numerator and denominator. This ratio may also be calculated with profit stated after deduction of tax.

Strategic and Organisational
Management

balanced scorecard approach   Approach to the provision of information to the management to assist strategic policy formulation and achievement. It emphasises the need to provide the user with a set of information which addresses all relevant areas of performance in an objective and unbiased fashion. The information provided may include both financial and non-financial elements, and cover areas such as profitability, customer satisfaction, internal efficiency and innovation.

barrier to entry   Any impediment to the free entry of new competitors into a market.

barrier to exit   Any impediment to the exit of existing competitors from a market.

benchmarking   Establishment, through data gathering, of targets and comparators, that permit relative levels of performance (and particularly areas of underperformance) to be identified. Adoption of identified best practices should improve performance.

internal benchmarking   Comparing one operating unit or function with another within the same industry.

functional benchmarking   Comparing internal functions with those of the best external practitioners, regardless of their industry (also known as operational benchmarking or generic benchmarking).

competitive benchmarking   In which information is gathered about direct competitors through techniques such as reverse engineering.

strategic benchmarking   Type of competitive benchmarking aimed at strategic action and organisational change.

Boston Consulting Group matrix
A representation of an entity's product or service offerings which shows the value of each product's sales expressed in relation to the growth rate of the market served and the market share held. The objective of the matrix is to assist in the allocation of funds to products. Products can be classified as star, cash cow, problem child or dog, according to their position on the matrix. *See* Figure 2.1.

business process re-engineering   Selection of areas of business activity in which repeatable and repeated sets of activities are undertaken, and the development of improved understanding of how they operate and of the scope for radical redesign with a view to creating and delivering better customer value.

FIGURE 2.1 BOSTON CONSULTING GROUP MATRIX

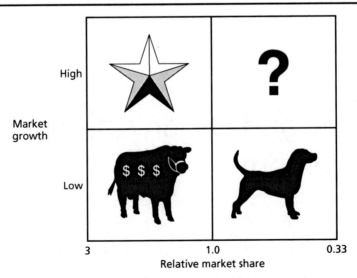

Relative market share

call off System whereby stock is held at the customer's premises, to be invoiced only on use.

cash cow Product characterised by a high market share but low market growth, whose function is seen as generating cash for use elsewhere within the entity.

competitive advantage Situation where an organisation exerts more competitive force on its competitors than they exert on it. *See* Porter's five forces.

competitive forces *See* Porter's five forces.

competitor analysis Identification and quantification of the relative strengths and weaknesses (compared with competitors or potential competitors), which could be of significance in the development of a successful competitive strategy.

contingency plan A plan, formulated in advance, to be implemented upon the occurrence of certain specific future events.

continuous improvement Derived from the Japanese term *kaizen*. A simple idea but when taken seriously over a period can lead to significant improvements. *See* kaizen.

corporate appraisal Critical assessment of the strengths and weaknesses, opportunities and threats (*SWOT analysis*) in relation to the internal and environmental factors affecting an entity in

order to establish its condition prior to the preparation of the long-term plan.

cost-volume-profit analysis (CVP) Study of the effects on future profit of changes in fixed cost, variable cost, sales price, quantity and mix.

critical success factor An element of organisational activity which is central to its future success. Critical success factors may change over time, and may include items such as product quality, employee attitudes, manufacturing flexibility and brand awareness.

customer account profitability Method of analysing the profits of an organisation by attributing costs and revenues to customers, rather than to products (as in direct product profitability).

customer relationship management (CRM) A culture, possibly supported by appropriate information systems, where emphasis is placed on the interfaces between the entity and its customers. Knowledge is shared, within the entity, to ensure that the customer receives a consistently high service level.

decision tree Pictorial method of showing a sequence of interrelated decisions and their expected outcomes. Decision trees can incorporate both the probabilities of, and values of, expected outcomes, and are used in decision making. *See* Figure 2.2.

FIGURE 2.2 DECISION TREE

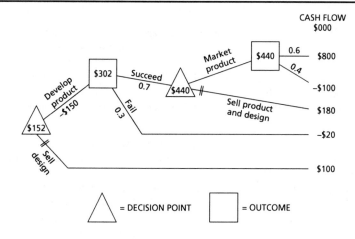

CASH FLOW $000

The decision tree shows the cash flows associated with the activities of (i) developing a product and (ii) selling the design. Problems are solved using decision trees by working from right to left. The decision tree on the left shows that the optimum course of action is to develop the product, generating a cash flow of $152,000, which is better than the alternative of selling the design, which generates $100,000.

△ = DECISION POINT   ☐ = OUTCOME

downsizing   Organisational restructuring involving outsourcing activities, replacing permanent staff with contract employees and reducing the number of levels within the organisational hierarchy, with the intention of making the entity more flexible, efficient and responsive to its environment.

economic order quantity (EOQ)   Most economic stock replenishment order size, which minimises the sum of stock ordering costs and stockholding costs. EOQ is used in an "optimising" stock control system.

EOQ may be calculated as:

$$\sqrt{\frac{2\,C_o\,D}{C_h}}$$

Where
D is demand for a time period
C_o is the cost of placing one order
C_h is the cost of holding one item for that time period

economy   Acquisition of resources of appropriate quantity and quality at minimum cost. *See* Figure 2.3.

FIGURE 2.3 ECONOMY, EFFECTIVENESS AND EFFICIENCY

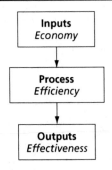

effectiveness   Utilisation of resources such that the output of the activity achieves the desired result. *See* Figure 2.3.

efficiency   Achievement of either maximum useful output from the resources devoted to an activity or the required output from the minimum resource input. *See* Figure 2.3.

enterprise resource planning (ERP)
Software system designed to support and automate the business processes of medium and large enterprises. ERP systems are accounting oriented information systems which aid in identifying and planning the enterprise wide resources needed to resource, make, account for and deliver customer orders.

Initially developed from MRP II systems, ERP tends to incorporate a number of software developments such as the use of relational databases, object-oriented programming and open system portability.

environmental impact assessment   Study which considers potential environmental effects during the planning phase before an investment is made or an operation started.

flexible manufacturing system (FMS)
Integrated, computer-controlled production system which is capable of producing any of a range of parts, and of switching quickly and economically between them.

forecast   A prediction of future events and their quantification for planning purposes.

gap analysis   A comparison between an entity's desired future performance level (most commonly expressed in terms of profit or ROCE) and the expected performance of projects both planned and underway. Differences are classified in a way which aids the understanding of performance, and which facilitates improvement.

generic strategies   *See* three generic strategies.

goal congruence   In a control system, the state which leads the individuals or groups to take actions which are in their self-interest and also in the best interest of the entity. Goal incongruence exists when the interests of individuals or of groups associated with an entity are not in harmony.

intellectual capital   Knowledge which can be used to create value. Intellectual capital includes:
human resources   The collective skills, experience and knowledge of employees;

intellectual assets Knowledge which is defined and codified such as drawing, computer program or collection of data; and *intellectual property* Intellectual assets which can be legally protected such as patents and copyrights.

ISO 9000 Quality system standard which requires complying organisations to operate in accordance with a structure of written policies and procedures that are designed to ensure the consistent delivery of a product or service to meet customer requirements.

just-in-time (JIT) System whose objective is to produce or to procure products or components as they are required by a customer or for use, rather than for stock.
just-in-time system Pull system, which responds to demand, in contrast to a *push* system, in which stocks act as buffers between the different elements of the system such as purchasing, production and sales.
just-in-time production Production system which is driven by demand for finished products, whereby each component on a production line is produced only when needed for the next stage.
just-in-time purchasing Purchasing system in which material purchases are contracted so that the receipt and usage of material, to the maximum extent possible, coincide.

kaizen Japanese term for continuous improvement in all aspects of an entity's performance at every level. *See* continuous improvement.

lead time Time interval between the start of an activity or process and its completion, for example the time between ordering goods and their receipt, or between starting production of a product and its completion. The latter is also known as *process time*.

limiting factor or key factor Anything which limits the activity of an entity. An entity seeks to optimise the benefit it obtains from the limiting factor. Examples are a shortage of supply of a resource or a restriction on sales demand at a particular price. *See* bottleneck (Chapter 1).

mark-down Reduction in the selling price of damaged or slow-selling goods.

mark-up Addition to the cost of goods or services which results in a selling price.

market share An entity's sales of a product or service in a specified market expressed as a proportion of total sales by all entities offering that product or service to the market. A planning tool and a performance assessment ratio.

mission Fundamental objective(s) of an entity expressed in general terms.

mission statement Published statement, apparently of the entity's fundamental objective(s). This may or may not summarise the true mission of the entity.

MRP (material requirements planning) System that converts a production schedule into a listing of the materials and components required to meet that schedule, so that adequate stock levels are maintained and items are available when needed.

MRP II (manufacturing resource planning) Expansion of material requirements planning (MRP) to give a broader approach than MRP to the planning and scheduling of resources, embracing areas such as finance, logistics, engineering and marketing.

national competitive advantage (Porter's diamond) Theory and model, proposed by M. Porter, for identifying why entities may achieve a competitive advantage over their rivals by virtue of being based or domiciled in a particular country. Often known as Porter's diamond, due to the shape of the diagrammatic representation of the model.

network analysis Quantitative technique used in project control. The events and activities making up the whole project are represented in the form of a diagram.
critical event Any event which lies on the critical path.
critical path Longest path or paths through a network.
event Start or completion of an activity. In a network an event is represented by a small circle (a node), and an activity by an arrow.
project evaluation and review technique (PERT) Specification of all activities, events,

probabilities and constraints relating to a project from which a network is drawn, providing a model of the way the project should proceed.

slack/float time Time available for an activity over and above that required for its completion.

objectives, hierarchy of Arrangement of the objectives of an entity into a number of different levels, with the higher levels being more general and the lower more specific. These levels may be mission, goals, targets or, alternatively; strategic objectives, tactical objectives or operational objectives.

operations plans Fully detailed specifications by which individuals are expected to carry out the predetermined cycles of operations to meet sectoral objectives.

outsourcing Use of external suppliers as a source of finished products, components or services. This is also known as *contract manufacturing* or *subcontracting*.

Pareto (80/20) distribution Frequency distribution with a small proportion (for example, 20%) of the items accounting for a large proportion (for example, 80%) of the value/resources. Common occurrences are sales, when 80% of turnover may arise from 20% of customers; inventory, when 20% of the items comprise 80% of the value. *See* Figure 2.4.

planning Establishment of objectives, and the formulation, evaluation and selection of the policies, strategies, tactics and action required to achieve them. Planning comprises long-term/strategic planning and short-term/operational planning. The latter is usually for a period of up to one year.

capital funding planning Process of selecting suitable funds to finance long-term assets and working capital.

capital resource planning Process of evaluating and selecting long-term assets to meet strategies.

financial planning Planning the acquisition of funds to finance planned activities.

futuristic planning Planning for that period which extends beyond the planning horizon in the form of future expected

FIGURE 2.4 PARETO (80/20) DISTRIBUTION: INVENTORY

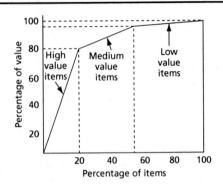

conditions which may exist in respect of the entity, products/services and environment but which cannot usefully be expressed in quantified terms. An example would be working out the actions needed in a future with no motor cars.

strategic planning Formulation, evaluation and selection of strategies for the purpose of preparing a long-term plan of action to attain objectives. Also known as *corporate planning* and *long-range planning*.

tactical planning Planning the utilisation of resources to achieve specific objectives in the most effective and efficient way.

planning horizon Furthest time ahead for which plans can be quantified. It need not be the planning period. *See* futuristic planning (planning).

planning period Period for which a plan is prepared and used. It differs according to the product or process life cycle. For example, forestry requires a period of many years whereas fashion garments require only a few months.

policy Undated, long-lasting and often unquantified statement of guidance regarding the way in which an organisation will seek to behave in relation to its stakeholders.

Porter's five forces External influences upon the extent of actual and potential competition within any industry which in aggregate determine the ability of firms within that industry to earn a profit. *See* Figure 2.5.

FIGURE 2.5 PORTER'S FIVE FORCES

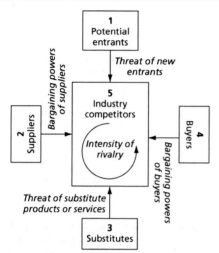

Porter's diamond   *See* national competitive advantage.

position audit   Part of the planning process which examines the current state of the entity in respect of: resources of tangible and intangible assets and finance; products, brands and markets; operating systems such as production and distribution; internal organisation; current results; and returns to stockholders.

pricing   Determination of a selling price for the product or service produced. A number of methodologies may be used including:
competitive pricing   Setting a price by reference to the prices of competitive products.
cost plus pricing   Determination of price by adding a mark-up, which may incorporate a desired return on investment, to a measure of the cost of the product/service.
dual pricing   Form of transfer pricing in which the two parties to a common transaction use different prices.
historical pricing   Basing current prices on prior period prices, perhaps uplifted by a factor such as inflation.

market-based pricing   Setting a price based on the value of the product in the perception of the customer. Also known as *perceived value pricing*.
penetration pricing   Setting a low selling price in order to gain market share.
predatory pricing   Setting a low selling price in order to damage competitors. May involve dumping, i.e. selling a product in a foreign market at below cost, or below the domestic market price (subject to, for example, adjustments for taxation differences, transportation costs, specification differences).
premium pricing   Achievement of a price above the commodity level, due to a measure of product or service differentiation.
price skimming   Setting a high price in order to maximise short-term profitability, often on the introduction of a novel product.
range pricing   Pricing of individual products such that their prices fit logically within a range of connected products offered by one supplier, and differentiated by a factor such as weight of pack or number of product attributes offered.
selective pricing   Setting different prices for the same product or service in different markets. Can be broken down as follows:
– *category pricing*   Cosmetically modifying a product such that the variations allow it to sell in a number of price categories, as where a range of "brands" are based on a common product.
– *customer group pricing*   Modifying the price of a product or service so that different groups of consumers pay different prices.
– *peak pricing*   Setting a price which varies according to level of demand.
– *service level pricing*   Setting a price based on the particular level of service chosen from a range.
– *time material pricing*   A form of cost-plus pricing in which price is determined by reference to the cost of the labour and material inputs to the product/service.

probability   Likelihood of an event or a state of nature occurring, being measured in a range from 0 (no possibility) to 1 (certainty).

product bundling   Form of discounting in which a group of related products is sold at a price which is lower than that obtainable by the consumer were the products to be purchased separately.

product life cycle   Period which begins with the initial product specification and ends with the withdrawal from the market of both the product and its support. It is characterised by defined stages including growth, development, introduction, maturity, decline and abandonment (CAM-I adapted).

programming
dynamic programming   Operational research technique used to solve multi-stage problems in which the decisions at one stage are the accepted assumptions applicable to the next stage.
linear programming   Series of linear equations used to construct a mathematical model. The objective is to obtain an optimal solution to a complex operational problem, which may involve the production of a number of products in an environment in which there are many constraints.
non-linear programming   Process in which the equations expressing the interactions of variables are not all linear but may, for example, be in proportion to the square of a variable.

projection   Expected future trend pattern obtained by extrapolation. It is principally concerned with quantitative factors, whereas a forecast includes judgements. *See* Figure 2.6.

quality assurance   Ensuring products or services consistently meet quality specifications.

re-order level   Level of stock at which a replenishment order should be placed. Traditional *optimising* systems use a variation on the following computation, which builds in a measure of safety stock and minimises the likelihood of a stock-out.

    (maximum usage × maximum lead time)

FIGURE 2.6   PROJECTION

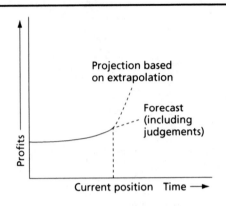

reverse engineering   Decomposition and analysis of competitors' products in order to determine how they are made, costs of production and the way in which future development may proceed.

risk   Condition in which there exists a quantifiable dispersion in the possible outcomes from any activity. Risk can be classified in a number of ways.

risk, business/operational   Relating to activities carried out within an entity, arising from structure, systems, people, products or processes.

risk, country   Associated with undertaking transactions with, or holding assets in, a particular country. Sources of risk might be political, economic or regulatory instability affecting overseas taxation, repatriation of profits, nationalisation or currency instability.

risk, environmental   Occurring due to changes in political, economic, socio-cultural, technological, environment and legal factors.

risk, financial   Relating to the financial operation of an entity and includes:
credit risk   Possibility that a loss may occur from the failure of another party to perform according to the terms of a contract.
currency risk   Risk that the value of a financial instrument will fluctuate due to changes in foreign exchange rates (IAS 32).

interest rate risk   Risk that interest rate changes will affect the financial well-being of an entity.

liquidity risk   Risk that an entity will encounter difficulty in realising assets or otherwise raising funds to meet commitments associated with financial instruments – this is also known as *funding risk*.

risk management   Process of understanding and managing the risks that the entity is inevitably subject to in attempting to achieve its corporate objectives. For management purposes, risks are usually divided into categories such as operational; financial; legal compliance; information and personnel. One example of an integrated solution to risk management is enterprise risk management. *See* risk management, enterprise.

risk management, enterprise (ERM)   Process effected by an entity's board of directors, management and other personnel, applied in strategy setting and across the enterprise, designed to identify potential events that may affect the entity, and manage risk to be within its risk appetite, to provide reasonable assurance regarding the achievement of entity objectives (Enterprise Risk Management – Integrated Framework COSO, 2004).

risk, market/systematic   Risk that cannot be diversified away, also known as *systematic risk*, which is measured by beta.
   Non-systematic or *unsystematic risk* applies to a single investment or class of investments, and can be reduced or eliminated by diversification.
   See market risk premium and beta factor.

risk, reputation   Damage to an entity's reputation as a result of failure to manage other risks.

rolling forecast   Continuously updated forecast whereby each time actual results are reported, a further forecast period is added and intermediate period forecasts are updated. *See* budget, rolling/continuous (Chapter 1).

sensitivity analysis   Modelling and risk assessment procedure in which changes are made to significant variables in order to determine the effect of these changes on the planned outcome. Particular attention is thereafter paid to variables identified as being of special significance.

shadow price   Increase in value which would be created by having available one additional unit of a limiting resource at its original cost. This represents the opportunity cost of not having the use of the one extra unit. This information is routinely produced when mathematical programming (especially linear programming) is used to model activity.

Six Sigma   Methodology, developed by Motorola others, based on Total Quality Management, to achieve very low defect rates. The "sigma" refers to the Greek letter used to denote standard deviation, so six sigma means that the error rate lies beyond six standard deviations from the mean. To achieve six sigma, an organisation must therefore produce not more than 3.4 defects per million products. *See* total quality management.

slack variables   Amount of each resource which will be unused if a specific linear programming solution is implemented.

stakeholders   Those persons and organisations that have an interest in the strategy of an organisation. Stakeholders normally include shareholders, customers, staff and the local community.

stock, buffer   Stock of materials, or of work-in-progress, maintained in order to protect user departments from the effect of possible interruptions to supply.

stock control   Systematic regulation of stock levels. Called *inventory control* in the US.

stock, free   Stock on hand or on order which has not been scheduled for use.
   (physical stock + stock ordered − stock scheduled for use)

stock level, maximum   Stock level, set for control purposes, which actual stockholding should never exceed.
   ((reorder level + EOQ) − (minimum rate of usage × minimum lead time))

stock level, minimum Stock level, set for control purposes, below which stockholding should not fall without being highlighted.

(reorder level – (average rate of usage × average lead time))

stock, safety Quantity of stocks of raw materials, work-in-progress and finished goods which are carried in excess of the expected usage during the lead time of an activity. The safety stock reduces the probability of operations having to be suspended.

strategic management accounting Form of management accounting in which emphasis is placed on information which relates to factors external to the entity, as well as non-financial information and internally generated information.

strategic plan Statement of long-term goals along with a definition of the strategies and policies which will ensure achievement of these goals.

strategy Course of action, including the specification of resources required, to achieve a specific objective. *See* Figure 1.10 (Chapter 1).

strategy map/mapping Diagram that describes how an entity creates value by linking the strategic objectives of an organisation in explicit cause and effect relationships within the four quadrants of the balanced scorecard.

SWOT analysis SWOT analysis, or corporate appraisal, evaluates the strategic position of an entity within its environment. Factors identified are listed as Strengths, Weaknesses, Opportunities or Threats.

tableau de bord Performance measurement approach, similar to the balanced scorecard, but developed and commonly used in France. A tableau de bord is a dashboard, such as that found in a car or aircraft. The tableau, in strategic management, sets out the various performance indicators in related groups.

tactical plan/tactics Short-term plan for achieving an entity's objectives. *See* Figure 1.10 (Chapter 1).

three generic strategies Strategies of differentiation, focus and cost leadership outlined by Porter as offering possible means of outperforming competitors within an industry, and of coping with the five competitive forces. *See* Porter's five forces. *See* Figure 2.7.

total quality management (TQM) Integrated and comprehensive system of planning and controlling all business functions so that products or services are produced which meet or exceed customer expectations.

TQM is a philosophy of business behaviour, embracing principles such as employee involvement, continuous improvement at all levels and customer focus, as well as being a collection of related techniques aimed at improving quality such as full documentation of activities, clear goal-setting and performance measurement from the customer perspective.

value chain Sequence of business activities by which, in the perspective of the end-user, value is added to the products or services produced by an entity.

FIGURE 2.7 PORTER'S THREE GENERIC STRATEGIES

| | | Competitive advantage | |
		Lower cost	Differentiation
Competitive scope	Broad target	1 Cost leadership	2 Differentiation
	Narrow target	3A Cost focus	3B Differentiation focus

Source: Reprinted with the permission of the Free Press, a Division of Simon & Schuster Adult Publishing Group, from COMPETITIVE ADVANTAGE: Creating and Sustaining Superior Performance by Michael E. Porter. Copyright © 1985, 1998 by Michael E. Porter. All rights reserved.

value for money Performance of an activity in such a way as to simultaneously achieve economy, efficiency and effectiveness.

value system Series of connected value chains belonging to the entity, its suppliers, rivals and customers.

value-added activity Activity necessary to enhance customer perceived value in the good or service being provided. The procurement of high quality resource inputs would be a value-adding activity while activity required to correct errors would be non-value-added in nature.

value-chain analysis Use of the value-chain model to identify the value adding activities of an entity.

vision statement *See* mission statement.

world-class manufacturing Position of international manufacturing excellence, achieved by developing a culture based on factors such as continuous improvement, problem prevention, zero defect tolerance, customer-driven JIT-based production and total quality management.

Governance and Compliance

Please note: Comparative figures have not been included in Figures 3.2, 3.3, 3.5, 3.6, 3.7, 3.8, 3.9 however IAS 1 prescribes that comparative information should be disclosed in respect of the previous period for all amounts reported in the financial statements.

account   Structured record of transactions in monetary terms kept as part of an accounting system. This may be a simple list, or entries on a debit and credit basis, maintained either manually or as a computer record. *See* Figure 3.1 for an illustration of the relationship of accounts.

cash account   Record of receipts and payments of cash, cheques or other forms of money transfer.

nominal account   Record of revenues and expenditures, liabilities and assets classified by their nature, for example sales, rent, rates, electricity, wages and share capital. These are sometimes referred to as impersonal accounts.

personal account   Record of amounts receivable from or payable to a person or an entity. A collection of these accounts is known as a *sales/debtor ledger*, or a *purchases/creditors ledger*. In the US the terms *receivables ledger* and *payables ledger* are used and are consistent with IAS 1.

accounting policies   Specific principles, bases, conventions, rules and practices applied by an entity in preparing and presenting its financial statements (IAS 8).

accounting reference period   Period for which an entity prepares its financial statements. This period is normally, though not necessarily, twelve months. Also used for taxation where it represents the period upon which adjusted profits, for corporation/income tax purposes, is based.

accounting standards   *See* International Financial Reporting Standards (IFRSs), which includes International Accounting Standards (IASs). In the UK there are Statements of Standard Accounting Practice (SSAPs) and Financial Reporting Standards (FRSs). All International and UK Accounting Standards are listed in Appendices 1 and 2.

Accounting Standards Board (ASB)
UK standard-setting body established to develop, issue and withdraw accounting standards. Its aims are to establish and improve standards of financial accounting and reporting, for the benefit of users, preparers and auditors of financial information (ASB). It will work with and influence the International Accounting Standards Board (IASB) in addressing UK accounting issues.

accruals basis of accounting   Effects of transactions and other events are recognised in financial statements when they occur and not when cash and cash equivalents are received or paid (IASB Framework).

FIGURE 3.1 RELATIONSHIP OF ACCOUNTS

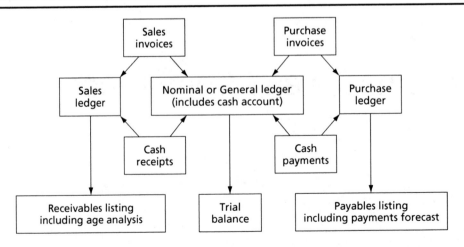

acquisition date   Date on which the acquirer effectively obtains control of the acquiree (IFRS 3).

actuarial assumptions   An entity's unbiased best estimates of the demographic and financial variables that will determine the ultimate cost of providing post-employment benefits (IAS 19).

administrative expenses   Cost of management, secretarial, accounting and other services which cannot be related to the separate production, marketing or research and development functions. These expenses are reported in the income statement.

amortisation   Systematic allocation of the depreciable amount of an asset over its useful life (IAS 36). Normally applied to intangible assets and goodwill.

amortised cost (for a financial asset or liability)   Amount at which the financial asset or liability is measured, at initial recognition minus principal repayments, plus or minus cumulative amortisation using the effective interest in the item (refer to IAS 39).

analytical review   An audit technique used to help analyse data to identify trends, errors, fraud, inefficiency and inconsistency. Its purpose is to understand what has happened in a system, to compare this with a standard and to identify weaknesses in practice or unusual situations that may require further investigation. The main methods of analytical review are ratio analysis, non-financial performance analysis, internal and external benchmarking and trend analysis. While the purpose of analytical review in external audit is to understand financial perormance and position and to identify areas for more in-depth audit treatment, analytical review in internal audit aims to better understand the control environment and identify potential control weaknesses.

annual report and accounts   Package of information including a management report, an auditor's report and a set of financial statements with supportive notes. In the case of companies these are drawn up for a period which is called the accounting reference period, the last day of which is known as the reporting date.

anti-dilution   Increase in earnings per share, or a reduction in loss per share, resulting from the assumption that convertible instruments are converted or options or warrants are exercised (refer to IAS 33). Also *see* dilution.

appropriation account   Record of how the surplus/deficit of a period has been allocated to distributions to owners and retentions by the entity.

asset   Resource controlled by the entity as a result of past events and from which future economic benefits are expected to flow to the entity (IAS 38).

associate   An entity, including an unincorporated entity such as a partnership, over which the investor has significant influence and that is neither a subsidiary nor an interest in a joint venture (refer to IAS 28).

audit   Systematic examination of the activities and status of an entity, based primarily on investigation and analysis of its systems, controls and records.

audit, compliance   Audit of specific activities in order to determine whether performance is in conformity with a predetermined contractual, regulatory or statutory requirement.

audit, cost   Verification of cost records and accounts, and a check on adherence to prescribed cost accounting procedures and their continuing relevance.

audit, environmental   Systematic, documented, periodic and objective evaluation of how well an entity, its management and equipment are performing with the aim of helping to safeguard the environment by facilitating management control of environmental practices and assessing compliance with entity policies and external regulations.

audit, internal   Independent appraisal function established within an organisation to examine and evaluate its activities as a service to the organisation. The objective of internal auditing is to assist members of the organisation in the effective discharge of their responsibilities. To this end, internal auditing furnishes them with analyses, appraisals, recommendations, counsel and information concerning the activities reviewed (Institute of Internal Auditors – UK).

audit, management   Objective and independent appraisal of the effectiveness of managers and the corporate structure in the achievement of entity objectives and policies. Its aim is to identify existing and potential management weaknesses and to recommend ways to rectify them.

audit, post-completion   Objective, independent assessment of the success of a capital project in relation to plan. Covers the whole life of the project and provides feedback to managers to aid the implementation and control of future projects.

audit report   Formal document in which an auditor expresses an opinion as to whether the financial statements of an entity show a true and fair view of its position at a given date and the results of its operations for the accounting period ended on that date have been properly prepared in accordance with the relevant statutory requirements, accounting standards, or any report by an auditor in accordance with the terms of appointment.

audit, statutory external   Periodic examination of the books of accounts and records of an entity carried out by an independent third party (the auditor) to ensure that they have been properly maintained, are accurate and comply with established concepts, principles, accounting standards, legal requirements and give a true and fair view of the financial state of the entity.

audit trail   Linked chain of evidence which connects accounting information with the source document which verifies its validity.

audit, value for money   Investigation into whether proper arrangements have been made for securing economy, efficiency and effectiveness in the use of resources.

Auditing Practices Board (APB)   A body formed by an agreement between the six members of the Consultative Committee of Accountancy Bodies (CCAB), to be responsible for developing and issuing professional standards for auditors in the UK and the Republic of Ireland.

From 2005, the APB will no longer issue its own standards but require the adoption of International Standards of Auditing (ISAs) issued by the International Auditing and Assurance Standards Board (IAASB). *See* Consultative Committee of Accountancy Bodies.

available-for-sale financial assets   Non-derivative financial asset that is designated as being available for sale and not classified as loans and receivables, held-to-maturity investments, or financial assets held at fair value (IAS 39).

bad debt   Debt or trade receivable which is, or is considered to be, uncollectable and is, therefore, written off either as a charge to the income statement or against an existing doubtful debt provision. *See* doubtful debts provision.

balance (on an account)   Difference between the totals of the debit and credit entries in an account.

balance sheet   Statement of the financial position of an entity at a given date disclosing the assets, liabilities and equity (such as shareholders' contributions and reserves) prepared to give a true and fair view of the entity at that date. *See* Figure 3.2.

bookkeeping   Recording of monetary transactions, appropriately classified, in the financial records of an entity. *See* double-entry bookkeeping.

business combination   Bringing together of separate entities or businesses into one reporting entity (IFRS 3). In all business combinations, one entity (the acquirer) will obtain control of another entity (the acquiree) and an acquirer should be

FIGURE 3.2 GROUP BALANCE SHEET AT 31 DECEMBER 2005 (REFER TO IAS 1)

	$ million	$ million
Assets		
Non-current assets		
Property, plant and equipment	1,503	
Investment properties	94	
Goodwill	356	
Other intangible assets	288	
Investments in associates and joint ventures	810	
Available-for-sale investments	68	3,119
Current assets		
Inventories	636	
Trade and other receivables	917	
Other current assets	291	
Cash and cash equivalents	104	1,948
Total assets		5,067
Equity and liabilities		
Equity attributable to equity holders of the parent		
Share capital	1,150	
Other reserves	452	
Translation reserve	(12)	
Retained earnings	434	2,024
Minority interest		246
Total equity		2,270
Non-current liabilities		
Long-term borrowings	1,030	
Deferred tax	320	
Long-term provisions	310	
Total non-current liabilities		1,660
Current liabilities		
Trade and other payables	477	
Short-term borrowings	283	
Current portion of long-term borrowings	82	
Current tax payable	125	
Short-term provisions	170	
Total current liabilities		1,137
Total liabilities		2,797
Total equity and liabilities		5,067

identified for all such combinations. (This means all business combinations involving an acquirer and an acquiree should be accounted for by applying the purchase (acquisition) method. The uniting of interests' (merger) method is now abolished.) Refer to IFRS 3.

business segment Distinguishable component of an entity that is engaged in providing an individual product or service (or group of products or services) and that is subject to risks and returns that are different from those of other segments (IAS 14). *See* geographic segment.

capital expenditure Costs incurred in acquiring, producing or enhancing non-current assets (both tangible and intangible). *See* revenue expenditure.

capital gain/loss Extent by which the net realised value of a capital asset exceeds (or in the case of a capital loss is less than) the cost of acquisition plus additional improvements, less depreciation charges where applicable. It can also arise from the exchange of such an asset for another of a different type. The term can have other interpretations for tax purposes.

capital maintenance Principle that profit is only recorded after capital has been maintained intact. There are two bases on which capital can be defined, financial and physical.

capital redemption reserve Account required to prevent a reduction in capital, where an entity purchases or redeems its own shares out of distributable profits.

capital surplus Assets remaining in an entity after all costs and liabilities have been discharged. It is distributed amongst the shareholders in accordance with the rights as determined at the time of the issue of shares.

capitalisation Recognising a cost as part of the cost of an asset (IAS 23). The asset will be included in the balance sheet as a non-current asset.

carrying amount Amount at which an asset is recognised in the balance sheet after deducting any accumulated depreciation (or amortisation) and accumulated impairment losses thereon (IAS 36).

cash Cash on hand and demand deposits (IAS 7).

cash equivalents Short-term, highly liquid investments that are readily convertible to known amounts of cash and which are subject to insignificant risk of changes in value (IAS 7).

cash flow statement Summarises the inflows and outflows of cash (and cash equivalents) for a period, classified under the following headings: operating activities, investing activities and financing activities (refer to IAS 7). *See* Figure 3.3.

cash generating unit Smallest identifiable group of assets that generates cash inflows that are largely independent of the cash

inflows from other assets or groups of assets (IAS 36).

chart of accounts Comprehensive and systematically arranged list of the named and numbered accounts applicable to an entity. *See* Figure 3.4.

closing rate Spot exchange rate (a rate for immediate delivery) at the balance sheet date (IAS 21).

code of ethics Set of standards governing the conduct of members of a certain profession, by specifying expected standards for competence, professional behaviour and integrity.

All members of the International Federation Accountants (IFAC) are expected to model their ethical codes on the IFAC code. There is therefore a specific ethical code for CIMA members.

commitment accounting Method of accounting which recognises expenditure as soon as it is contracted.

committee, audit Formally constituted committee of an entity's main board of directors whose responsibilities include: monitoring the integrity of any formal announcements on financial performance including financial statements; reviewing internal financial controls, internal control and risk management systems; monitoring the effectiveness of the internal audit function; making recommendations in respect of the appointment or removal of the external auditor; reviewing and monitoring auditor independence and the effectiveness of the audit process.

committee, nominations Formally constituted committee of an entity's main board of directors. The committee's main functions are to establish the criteria for board membership, identify suitable candidates and make recommendations for appointment to the Board.

committee, remuneration Formally constituted committee of an entity's main board of directors whose primary function is to consider the performance and

FIGURE 3.3 GROUP CASH FLOW STATEMENT FOR THE YEAR ENDED 31 DECEMBER 2005 [Indirect method] (REFER TO IAS 7)

	$ million	$ million
Cash flows from operating activities		
Profit before tax	403	
Adjustments for		
Depreciation	80	
Finance costs	85	
Finance income	(56)	
Share of profits of associates and joint ventures	(147)	
	365	
Increase in inventories	(49)	
Decrease in trade and other receivables	63	
Increase in trade and other payables	41	
Cash generated from operations	420	
Finance costs paid	(30)	
Income taxes paid	(137)	
Net cash from operating activities		253
Cash flows from investing activities		
Purchase of property, plant and equipment	(273)	
Proceeds from sale of property and equipment	110	
Finance income received	16	
Dividends received from investments	92	
Net cash used in investing activities		(55)
Cash flows from financing activities		
Proceeds from issue of share capital	125	
Repayments of long-term borrowings	(75)	
Equity dividends paid (see note below)	(70)	
Net cash used in financing activities		(20)
Net increase in cash and cash equivalents		178
Cash and cash equivalents at 1 January 2005		(74)
Cash and cash equivalents at 31 December 2005		104

Note: Alternatively, equity dividends paid may be shown as cash flow from operating activities.

FIGURE 3.4 EXTRACT FROM CHART OF ACCOUNTS

Code	Account descriptor
1	Assets
2	Liabilities
3	Equity
4	Expenses
5	Revenue
11	Non-current assets
12	Current assets
111	Land
112	Buildings
113	Plant
114	Motor vehicles

remuneration of the executive directors. Remuneration issues will include performance-related payments, pension rights, compensation payments and share option schemes.

component of an entity Operations and cash flows that can be clearly distinguished operationally, and for financial reporting purposes, from the rest of the entity (IFRS 5).

compound instrument Financial instrument that, from the issuer's perspective, contains both a liability and an equity element (IAS 32).

consignment inventory Inventory held by one party (the dealer) but legally owned by another (the manufacturer) on terms that may give the dealer the right to sell the inventory in the normal course of business or, at the dealer's option, return it unsold to the manufacturer.

consolidated financial statements Financial statements of a group presented as those of a single economic entity (IAS 27).

construction contract Specifically negotiated for the construction of an asset or a combination of assets that are closely inter-related or inter-dependent in terms of their design, technology and function or their ultimate purpose or use (IAS 11).

constructive obligation Obligation that derives from an entity's actions where:
(a) by an established pattern of past practice, published policies or a sufficiently specific current statement, the entity has indicated to other parties that it will accept certain responsibilities; and
(b) as a result, the entity has created a valid expectation on the part of those other parties that it will discharge those responsibilities (IAS 37).

Consultative Committee of Accountancy Bodies (CCAB) A forum (now a limited company) in which matters affecting the six member bodies and the UK and Irish professions as a whole can be discussed and co-ordinated, thus allowing the profession to speak with a unified voice to the UK and Irish governments. The six member bodies are ACCA, CIMA, CIPFA, ICAEW, ICAI and ICAS.

contingent asset Possible asset that arises from past events and whose existence will be confirmed only by the occurrence of one or more uncertain future events not wholly within the control of the entity (IAS 37).

contingent liability
(a) A possible obligation that arises from past events and whose existence will be confirmed only by the occurrence or non-occurrence of one or more uncertain future events not wholly within the entity's control; or
(b) A present obligation that arises from past events but is not recognised because it is not probable that a transfer of economic benefits will be required to settle the obligation; or the amount of the obligation cannot be measured with sufficient reliability (IAS 37).

continuing operation *See* discontinued operation.

control (in the context of an asset) Ability to obtain the future economic benefits relating to an asset and to restrict the access of others to these benefits.

control (of an entity) Power to govern the financial and operating policies of an entity so as to obtain benefits from its activities (IAS 27).

convertible debt Liability that gives the holder the right to convert into another instrument, normally ordinary shares at a predetermined price/rate and time.

corporate social accounting Reporting of the social and environmental impact of an entity's activities upon those who are directly associated with the entity (for instance, employees, customers, suppliers) or those who are in any way affected by the activities of the entity, as well as an assessment of the cost of compliance with relevant regulations in this area.

corporation tax Tax chargeable on companies resident in the UK or trading in the UK. Referred to internationally as income tax.

cost of sales The cost of goods sold during an accounting period. For a retail business this will be the cost of goods available for sale (opening stock plus purchases) minus closing stock. For a manufacturing business it will include all direct and indirect production costs.

creative accounting Form of accounting which, while complying with all regulations and practices, nevertheless gives a biased impression (generally favourable) of an entity's financial performance and position. *See* window-dressing.

creditor *See* payables.

current account Record of transactions between two parties. For example, between a bank and its customer or a branch and its head office.

current asset Asset which satisfies any of the following criteria:
(a) is expected to be realised in, or is intended for sale or consumption in, the entity's normal operating cycle;
(b) is held primarily for the purpose of being traded;
(c) is expected to be realised within twelve months of the balance sheet date; or
(d) is cash or cash equivalent (IAS 1).

current cost accounting (CCA) Method of accounting in which profit is defined as the surplus after allowing for price changes on the funds needed to continue the existing business and to maintain its operating capability, whether financed by shares or borrowing. A CCA balance sheet shows the effect of physical capital maintenance.

current liability Liability which satisfies any of the following criteria:
(a) is expected to be settled in the entity's normal operating cycle;
(b) is held primarily for the purpose of being traded; or
(c) is due to be settled within twelve months of the balance sheet date.
All other liabilities are classified as non-current (IAS 1).

current purchasing power accounting (CPP) Method of accounting in which the values of non-monetary items in the historical cost financial statements are adjusted, using a general price index, so that the resulting profit allows for the maintenance of the purchasing power of the shareholders' interest in the entity. A CPP balance sheet shows the effect of financial capital maintenance.

current tax Amount of income taxes payable (or recoverable) in respect of the taxable profit (or loss) for a period (IAS 12).

date of transition (to IFRSs) Beginning of the earliest period for which an entity presents full comparative information under IFRSs in its first IFRS-compliant financial statements (IFRS 1).

debtor *See* receivables.

deductible temporary difference Temporary difference that will result in amounts that are deductible in determining taxable profit (or tax loss) of future periods when the carrying amount of the asset or liability is recovered or settled (IAS 12).

deferred expenditure Expenditure not charged against income in an accounting period but carried forward as a non-current or current asset to be charged in one or more subsequent periods, for example development expenditure (refer to IAS 38).

deferred tax Difference between the tax ultimately payable on the profits recognised in an accounting period and the actual amount of tax payable for the same accounting period. The former figure will be based on the tax implications of accounting profit and the carrying amounts of assets and liabilities. The latter figure will be based on a calculation of profits as recognised by the tax authorities.

deferred tax asset Amount of income taxes recoverable in future periods in respect of deductible temporary differences, carried forward unused tax losses and unused tax credits (IAS 12).

deferred tax liability Amount of income taxes payable in future periods in respect of taxable temporary differences (IAS 12).

defined benefit plan Any post-employment scheme other than a defined contribution plan (IAS 19). In such a scheme the employer takes the risk – also known as a final salary scheme.

defined contribution plan Post-employment benefit plan under which an entity pays fixed contributions into a separate entity (the fund) and will have no legal or constructive obligation to pay further contributions, if the fund does not hold sufficient assets to pay all employee benefits relating to their service in the current and prior periods (IAS 19). In such a scheme the employee takes the risk – also known as a money purchase scheme.

depreciable amount Cost of an asset, or other amount substituted for cost, less the residual value (IAS 16).

depreciation Systematic allocation of the depreciable amount of an asset over its useful life (IAS 16). Normally applied to tangible assets. *See* amortisation.

deprival value Basis for valuing assets based on the maximum amount which an entity would be willing to pay rather than forgo the asset. Deprival value is the *lower of* replacement cost and recoverable amount (itself the *higher of* fair value less costs to sell and value in use). *See* impairment.

<pre>
              Deprival value
                    |
                 lower of
                  ⌒⌒⌒
Replacement Cost   Recoverable Amount
                            |
                        higher of
                         ⌒⌒⌒
              Fair Value less   Value in Use
              Costs to Sell
</pre>

de-recognition Removal of a previously recognised asset (or liability) from an entity's balance sheet.

development costs Costs incurred in applying research findings or other knowledge to a plan or design for the production of new or substantially improved materials, devices, products, processes, systems or services prior to the commencement of commercial production or use (IAS 38).

dilution Reduction in the earnings and voting power per share caused by an increase or potential increase in the number of shares in issue. For the purpose of calculating diluted earnings per share, the profit attributable to ordinary shareholders and the weighted average number of shares outstanding should be adjusted for the effects of all dilutive potential ordinary shares. Also *see* anti-dilution.

discontinued operation Component of an entity that has either been disposed of or is classified as held for sale and:
(a) represents, or is part of a single plan to dispose of, a separate major line of business or geographical area of operations; or
(b) is a subsidiary acquired exclusively with a view to resale (IFRS 5). *See* Figure 3.5.

disposal group Group of assets to be disposed of, by sale or otherwise, together as a group in a single transaction, and liabilities directly associated with those assets that will be transferred in the transaction (IFRS 5).

distributable reserves Profit for a period, plus retained earnings from previous periods, that are available for payment as dividends (or other distributions to owners). The split between distributable and non-distributable reserves is a UK legal requirement to ensure that creditors have some protection from the effects of losses.

distribution costs Cost of warehousing saleable products and delivering them to customers. These costs are reported in the income statement.

dividend Distribution of profits to the holders of equity investments in proportion to their holdings of a particular class of capital (IAS 18).

dominant influence Influence that can be exercised over an entity to achieve the operating and financial policies designed by the holder of the influence, notwithstanding the rights or influence of any other party.

double-entry bookkeeping/accounting Most commonly used system of bookkeeping based on the principle that every financial transaction involves the simultaneous receiving and giving of value, and is therefore recorded twice.

doubtful debts provision Amount charged against profit and deducted from trade receivables to allow for the estimated non-recovery of a proportion of the trade receivables. *See* bad debt.

FIGURE 3.5 PRESENTATION OF DISCONTINUED OPERATIONS (REFER TO IFRS 5)

GROUP INCOME STATEMENT FOR THE YEAR ENDED 31 DECEMBER 2005	Continuing operations $ million	Discontinued operations $ million	Totals $ million
Revenue	3,561	786	4,347
Cost of sales	(2,883)	(766)	(3,649)
Gross profit	678	20	698
Other operating income	73		73
Distribution costs	(241)	(11)	(252)
Administrative expenses	(142)	(31)	(173)
Other operating expenses	(61)		(61)
Profit (loss) from operations	307	(22)	285
Finance costs	(72)	(13)	(85)
Finance income	56		56
Share of profits of associates and joint ventures	147		147
Profit (loss) before tax	438	(35)	403
Income tax expense	(180)	11	(169)
Profit (loss) for the year	258	(24)	234

Alternative presentation

	$ million
Continuing operations	
Revenue	3,561
Cost of sales	(2,883)
Gross profit	678
Other operating income	73
Distribution costs	(241)
Administrative expenses	(142)
Other operating expenses	(61)
Profit (loss) from operations	307
Finance costs	(72)
Finance income	56
Share of profits of associates and joint ventures	147
Profit before tax	438
Income tax expense	(180)
Profit for the year from continuing operations	258
Discontinued operations	
Loss for the year from discontinued operations	(24)
Profit for the year	234

earnings per share, basic Profit for the period that is attributable to ordinary shareholders (the numerator) divided by the weighted average number of ordinary shares outstanding during the period (the denominator) (IAS 33).

earnings per share, diluted Basic earnings per share with both the numerator and the denominator adjusted for the effects of all dilutive potential ordinary shares (refer to IAS 33).

employee benefits All forms of consideration given by an entity in exchange for service rendered by employees (IAS 19).

entity Economic unit that has a separate, distinct identity, for example an industrial or commercial company (or enterprise), charity, local authority, government agency or fund.

environmental reporting Report or disclosure by an entity that discusses and/or quantifies the benefits and costs of the entity's interaction with its operating environment.

equity   Residual interest in the assets of the entity after deducting all its liabilities (IASB Framework). It is comprised of share capital, retained earnings and other reserves of a single entity, plus minority interests in a group, representing the investment made in the entity by its owners.

equity instrument   Contract that evidences a residual interest in the assets of an entity after deducting all of its liabilities (IAS 32).

equity method of accounting   Method of accounting whereby the investment is initially recognised at cost and adjusted thereafter for the post-acquisition change in the investor's share of the net assets of the investee. The profit or loss of the investor includes the investor's share of the profit or loss of the investee. A method used to account for associates and (optionally) joint ventures (refer to IAS 28 and IAS 31).

equity shares   *See* ordinary shares.

events after the balance sheet date   Events, favourable and unfavourable, that occur between the balance sheet date and the date the financial statements are authorised for issue.
adjusting events   Those that provide evidence of conditions that existed at the balance sheet date.
non-adjusting events   Those that are indicative of conditions that arose after the balance sheet date.
   (Refer to IAS 10).

exceptional items   Material items which derive from events or transactions that should be disclosed in the notes to the financial statements by virtue of their size or incidence in relation to the income statement.

fair value   Amount for which an asset could be exchanged, or a liability settled, between knowledgeable and willing parties in an arm's length transaction (IAS 2).

fair value less costs to sell   Amount obtainable from the sale of an asset (or cash generating unit) in an arm's length transaction between knowledgeable and willing parties, less the direct costs of disposal (IAS 36).

financial accounting   Classification and recording of the monetary transactions of an entity in accordance with established concepts, principles, accounting standards and legal requirements and their presentation, by means of income statements, balance sheets and cash flow statements, during and at the end of an accounting period.

financial position   Relationship of the assets, liability and equity of an entity as reported in its balance sheet (IASB Framework).

Financial Reporting Council (FRC)   UK's single independent regulator of financial reporting and corporate governance with delegated statutory powers. The FRC oversees the work of the Accounting Standards Board (ASB), the Financial Reporting Review Panel (FRRP), the Professional Oversight Board for Accountancy, the Auditing Practices Board (APB) and the Accountancy Investigation and Discipline Board.

Financial Reporting Review Panel   UK review panel established to examine contentious departures, by large companies, from accounting standards.

Financial Reporting Standard (FRS)   A UK accounting standard issued since 1 August 1990, when the Accounting Standards Board (ASB) succeeded the Accounting Standards Committee (ASC).

financial statements   Complete set of financial statements comprises: balance sheet, income statement, statement of changes in equity or statement of recognised income and expense, cash flow statement, notes comprising a summary of significant accounting policies and other explanatory notes.

financing activities   Activities that result in changes in the size and composition of the contributed equity and borrowings of an entity as reported in its cash flow statement (IAS 7).

fixed charge   Protection given to creditors whereby they can enforce the sale of specified (non-current) asset(s) if there is a default.

floating charge   Protection given to creditors whereby they can enforce the sale of any (non-current) asset(s) if there is a default.

foreign currency transaction   Transaction that is denominated in, or requires settlement in, a foreign currency (IAS 21).

foreign currency translation   Restatement of the transactions or financial statements of a foreign operation into the reporting currency of the parent (or investor) for the purpose of preparing consolidated financial statements.

foreign operation   An entity that is a subsidiary, associate, joint venture or branch of the reporting entity, the activities of which are based or conducted in a country other than the country of the reporting entity (IAS 21).

forensic accounting   Use of accounting records and documents in order to determine the legality or otherwise of past activities.

FRSSE   Financial Reporting Standard for Smaller Entities. This is a single standard for an optional simplified reporting regime for smaller entities in the UK.

fungible assets   Assets which are substantially indistinguishable one from another, for example a holding of shares in an entity.

generally accepted accounting practice (GAAP)   Components of UK GAAP include: the provisions of company law; the accounting standards issued by the ASB; UITF Abstracts; Statements of Recommended Practice; stock exchange listing roles; professional recommendations and pronouncements of the Financial Reporting Review Panel. For matters not covered by these, the practices of leading companies and audit firms are widely accepted as possessing authority.

geographic segment   Distinguishable component of an entity that is engaged in providing products or services within a particular economic environment and that is subject to risks and returns that are different from those of components operating in other economic environments (IAS 14). *See* business segment.

goodwill
acquired   Future economic benefits arising from assets that are not capable of being individually identified and separately recognised (refer to IFRS 3).
positive goodwill   Excess of the purchase consideration over the fair value of the identifiable net assets acquired.
negative goodwill   Excess of the fair value of the identifiable net assets acquired over the purchase consideration.
internally generated   An entity's own view of its value above its recorded value which cannot be recognised in financial statements prepared in accordance with accounting standards.

Governance, Combined Code on Corporate   Guidance on good governance for UK listed companies, published in July 2003 and consolidating earlier voluntary corporate governance codes (Cadbury, Greenbury, Hampel, Higgs and Smith). The Combined Code is annexed to the Listing Rules of the UK Listing Authority, the FSA (Financial Services Authority). Listed companies are required to state whether they comply with the Code, and justify any departures.

governance, corporate   The system by which companies and other entities are directed and controlled. The boards of directors are responsible for the governance of their companies and other entities. The shareholders' role in governance is to appoint the directors and the auditors, and to satisfy themselves that an appropriate governance structure is in place. The responsibilities of the board include setting the company's (or entity's) strategic aims, providing the leadership to put them into effect, supervising the management of the company (or entity) and reporting to shareholders on their stewardship. The board's actions are subject to laws, regulations and the shareholders in general meeting.

governance, enterprise   Set of responsibilities and practices exercised by the board and executive management with the goal of providing strategic direction, ensuring that objectives are achieved, ascertaining that risks are managed appropriately and verifying that the organisation's resources are used responsibly (Information Systems Audit and Control Foundation.

Governance, OECD Principles of Corporate Framework for good practice which has been agreed by the governments of all OECD member countries. They have been designed to assist governments and regulatory bodies in both OECD countries and elsewhere in drawing up and enforcing effective rules, regulations and codes of corporate governance. In parallel, they provide guidance for stock exchanges, investors, companies (and other entities) and others that have a role in the process of developing good corporate governance.

government grants Assistance by the government (including local, national and international agencies) in the form of transfer of resources to an entity in return for past or future compliance with certain conditions relating to the operating activities of the entity (IAS 20).

group A parent and all its subsidiaries (IAS 27).

group accounts *See* consolidated financial statements.

hedge effectiveness Degree to which changes in the fair value or cash flows of the hedged item that are attributable to a hedged risk are offset by changes in the fair value or cash flows of the hedging instrument (IAS 39).

hedged instrument Designated derivative whose fair value or cash flows are expected to offset changes in the fair value or cash flows of a designated hedged item (IAS 39).

hedged item Asset, liability, firm commitment, highly probable forecast transaction or net investment in a foreign operation that exposes the entity to risks of changes in fair value or future cash flows and is designated as being hedged (IAS 39).

held-to-maturity investment Non-derivative financial assets with fixed or determinable payments and fixed maturity that an entity has the positive intention and ability to hold to maturity (IAS 39).

historical cost For assets – recorded at the amount of cash (or cash equivalents) paid or the fair value of the consideration given to acquire them at the time of their acquisition.

For liabilities – recorded at the amount of proceeds received in exchange for the obligation (for example, income taxes) or at the amounts of cash (or cash equivalents) expected to be paid to satisfy the liability in the normal course of business.

(Refer to IASB Framework)

historical cost accounting System of accounting in which all values are based on the historical costs incurred.

horizontal group Position where two or more undertakings are controlled by a common parent, such as a private individual, who is not subject to the requirements of regulations or corporate laws. There is therefore no legal or professional mechanism which can be used to require the preparation of consolidated financial statements. *See* consolidated financial statements.

human resource accounting Identification, recording and reporting of the investment in, and return from the employment of, the personnel of an entity.

hyperinflation Loss of purchasing power of money at such a rate that comparison of amounts from transactions and other events that have occurred at different times, even within the same accounting period, is misleading (IAS 29). As an indication, hyperinflation could exist where the cumulative inflation rate over three years is 100%.

identifiable assets and liabilities Assets and liabilities of an entity that are capable of being disposed of or settled separately, without disposing of a business of the entity (FRS 10).

impairment Reduction in the carrying value of a non-current asset where its recoverable amount (the higher of fair value less costs to sell and value in use) is less than its existing carrying amount.

imprest system Method of controlling cash or inventory. When the cash or inventory has been reduced by disbursements or issues it is restored to its original level.

inception of a lease Earlier of the date of the lease agreement and the date of commitment by the parties to the principal provisions of the lease (IAS 17).

income Increases in economic benefits during an accounting period in the form of inflows or enhancements of assets, or decreases of liabilities that result in increases in equity, other than those relating to contributions from equity holders (IASB Framework).

income and expenditure account Financial statement for not-for-profit entities such as clubs, associations and charities. It shows the surplus or deficit, being the excess of income over expenditure or vice versa, for a period and is drawn up on the same accruals basis as an income statement.

income statement Financial statement including all the profits and losses recognised in a period, unless an accounting standard requires inclusion elsewhere (refer to IAS 1). *See* Figure 3.6.

FIGURE 3.6 GROUP INCOME STATEMENT FOR THE YEAR ENDED 31 DECEMBER 2005 (REFER TO IAS 1)

	$ million	$ million
Classifies expenses by function		
Revenue		4,347
Cost of sales		(3,649)
Gross profit		698
Other operating income	73	
Distribution costs	(252)	
Administrative expenses	(173)	
Other operating expenses	(61)	(413)
Profit from operations		285
Finance costs	(85)	
Finance income	56	
Share of profits of associates and joint ventures	147	118
Profit before tax		403
Income tax expense		(169)
Profit for the year		234
Attributable to		
Equity holders of the parent		199
Minority interests		35
Profit for the year		234

Alternative presentation

Classifies expenses by nature	$ million
Revenue	4,347
Other operating income	73
Changes in inventories of finished goods and work-in-progress	(42)
Work performed by the enterprise and capitalised	NIL
Raw materials and consumables used	(2,220)
Employee benefit costs	(1,539)
Depreciation and amortisation expense	(273)
Other operating expenses	(61)
Profit from operations	285

Thereafter the income statement is the same as above.

incomplete records   Accounting system which is not double-entry bookkeeping. Various degrees of incompleteness can occur, for example *single-entry bookkeeping*, in which usually only a cash book is maintained.

intangible assets   Identifiable non-monetary asset without physical substance which must be controlled by the entity as the result of past events and from which the entity expects a flow of future economic benefits (refer to IAS 38).

interim financial report   Financial report containing either a complete set of financial statements or a set of condensed financial statements for an interim period (one shorter than a full financial year) (refer to IAS 34).

internal check   Procedures designed to provide assurance that:
(a)   everything which should be recorded has been recorded;
(b)   errors or irregularities are identified; and
(c)   assets and liabilities exist and are correctly recorded.

internal control   Management system of controls, financial and otherwise, established in order to provide reasonable assurance of:
(a)   effective and efficient operation;
(b)   internal financial control; and
(c)   compliance with laws and regulations.
    Good internal control systems should make accounting records more reliable and the occurrence of fraud and error more difficult.

internal financial control   Internal controls established in order to provide reasonable assurance of:
(a)   the safeguarding of the entity's assets against unauthorised use or disposal; and
(b)   the maintenance of proper accounting records and the reliability of financial information used within the entity or for publication.

International Accounting Standards Board (IASB)   Has sole responsibility for the development and publication of IFRSs. Seeks to develop a single set of high quality global Accounting Standards requiring transparent and comparable information in general purpose financial statements. Over 90 countries will either require or permit the use of the IASB's Standards and Interpretations for domestically listed entities by 2007.
    Also *see* Standards Advisory Council (SAC) and International Financial Reporting Interpretations Committee (IFRIC).

International Accounting Standards Committee Foundation (IASCF)   Selects, oversees and funds the IASB and its two advisory bodies (IFRIC, SAC) under the direction of its Trustees.

International Auditing and Assurance Standards Board (IAASB)   Independent standard setting body under the auspices of the International Federation of Accountants (IFAC). The IAASB issues:
–   International Standards on Auditing (ISAs);
–   International Standards on Assurance Engagements (ISAEs);
–   International Standards on Related Services (ISRSs); and
–   International Standards on Quality Control (ISQCs).

International Financial Reporting Interpretations Committee (IFRIC)   Assists the IASB in improving standards of financial accounting and reporting. This is achieved by providing timely guidance on newly identified financial reporting issues not specifically addressed by IFRSs or where unsatisfactory or conflicting interpretations have developed or seem likely to develop.

International Financial Reporting Standards (IFRSs)   Standards and Interpretations published or adopted by the International Accounting Standards Board (IASB). They comprise:
–   International Financial Reporting Standards (IFRSs)
–   International Accounting Standards (IASs)
–   Interpretations originated by the International Financial Reporting

Interpretations Committee (IFRIC) or the former Standing Interpretations Committee (SIC). *See* Appendix 1 for a full list of current IASs and IFRSs.

inventories Assets held for sale in the ordinary course of business in the process of production for such a sale or in the form of materials or supplies to be consumed in the production process or in the rendering of services (IAS 2). Synonym for *stock*.

investing activities Acquisition and disposal of long-term (non-current) assets and other investments not included in cash equivalents as reported in the entity's cash flow statement (IAS 7).

investment Any application of funds which is intended to provide a return by way of interest, dividend or capital appreciation.

investment property Property (land or building or part of a building) held by the owner (or by the lessee under a finance lease) to earn rentals and/or for capital appreciation (IAS 40).

joint control – joint venture Contractually agreed sharing of control over an economic activity which exists only when the strategic and operating decisions relating to the activity require the unanimous consent of the parties sharing control (the venturers) (IAS 31).

joint control – related parties Contractually agreed sharing of control over an economic activity (IAS 24).

joint venture Contractual arrangement whereby two or more parties undertake an economic activity which is subject to joint control (IAS 31).

key management personnel Those persons having authority and responsibility for planning, directing and controlling the activities of the entity, directly or indirectly, including any director (whether executive or otherwise) of that entity (IAS 24).

legal obligation Obligation that derives from:
(a) contract (through its explicit or implicit terms);
(b) legislation;
(c) or other operation of law (IAS 37).

lease Agreement whereby the lessor conveys to the lessee, in return for a payment or series of payments, the right to use an asset for an agreed period of time (IAS 17).

lease term Non-cancellable period for which the lessee has contracted to lease the asset together with any further term for which the lessee has the option to continue to lease the asset, with or without further payment, which at the inception of the lease it is reasonably certain that the lessee will exercise (IAS 17).

lease, finance Lease agreement that transfers substantially all the risks and rewards incidental to ownership of an asset from the lessor to the lessee. Title in the asset may or may not eventually be transferred (IAS 17).

lease, operating Lease agreement other than a finance lease (IAS 17).

liability Present obligation of the entity arising from past events, the settlement of which is expected to result in an outflow from the entity of resources embodying economic benefits (IAS 37).

liability method Method of computing deferred tax by calculating it at the rate of income tax that it is estimated will be applied in the period when the temporary difference reverses. This means the liability is measured at the amount of income tax that it is estimated will be paid or recovered.

liquid assets Cash, cash equivalents and other assets readily convertible into cash, for example short-term investments.

loans and receivables Non-derivative financial assets with fixed or determinable payments that are not quoted in an active market (IAS 39).

Management's Discussion and Analysis (MD&A)   Narrative element of the statutory reporting package required in the US. It is intended to allow users to understand an entity's financial condition, changes in financial condition and results of operations, and is a discussion and analysis of the entity's operations and prospects, by management.

It should fulfil the following objectives:

(a)   to provide a narrative explanation of an entity's financial statements that enables investors to see the company through the eyes of its management;

(b)   to enhance the overall financial disclosure and provide the context within which financial information should be analysed; and

(c)   to provide information about the quality of, and potential variability of, an entity's earnings and cash flow, so that investors can ascertain the likelihood that past performance is indicative of future performance.

(SEC Statement About Management's Discussion & Analysis of Financial Condition and Results of Operations, Release No. 33-8056, 2002).

minority interest   Portion of the profit or loss (income statement) and net assets (balance sheet) of a subsidiary attributable to equity interests that are not owned, directly or indirectly, by the parent (IFRS 3).

monetary items   Units of currency held and assets and liabilities to be received or paid in a fixed or determinable number of units of currency (IAS 21).

money laundering   Funnelling of cash or other funds generated from illegal activities through legitimate financial institutions and businesses to conceal the source of the funds (Anti-Money Laundering, 2nd ed, IFAC, 2004).

net assets   Excess of the carrying amount of assets over liabilities. Equivalent to net worth or equity.

net book value   *See* carrying amount.

net realisable value (NRV)   *See* fair value less costs to sell.

non-current asset   Any asset that does not meet the definition of a current asset (IFRS 5). Tangible or intangible asset, acquired for retention by an entity for the purpose of providing a service to the entity and not held for resale in the normal course of trading. Previously known as a fixed asset.

non-executive director   Director of a company (or other entity) who is not involved in the day-to-day running of operations and is therefore expected to provide an independent view on board issues.

notes to financial statements   Contain information in addition to that presented in the balance sheet, income statement, statement of changes in equity and cash flow statement. Notes provide narrative descriptions or disaggregations of items disclosed in those statements and information about items that do not qualify for recognition in those statements (IAS 1).

obligating event   Event that creates a legal or constructive obligation that results in an entity having no realistic alternative to settling that obligation (IAS 37).

obsolescence   Loss of value of a non-current asset due to advances in technology or changes in market conditions for its product.

off balance sheet finance   Funding or refinancing of an entity's operations in such a way that, under existing legal requirements and accounting practices, some or all of the financing may not be shown on the entity's balance sheet.

onerous contract   Contract in which the unavoidable costs of meeting the obligations under the contract exceed the economic benefits expected to be received under it (IAS 37).

operating activities   The principal revenue-producing activities of an entity and other activities not reported elsewhere in the entity's cash flow statement (IAS 7).

Operating and Financial Review (OFR)   Narrative element of the statutory reporting package, from April 2005 required by law for listed companies in the UK.

It is a balanced and comprehensive analysis of:

(a) the development and performance of the business of the entity during the financial year;

(b) the position of the entity at the end of the year;

(c) the main trends and factors underlying the development, performance and position of the business of the entity during the financial year; and

(d) the main trends and factors which are likely to affect their future development, performance and position, prepared so as to assist investors to assess the strategies adopted by the entity and the potential for those strategies to succeed (ASB Reporting Standard 1: Operating and Financial Review).

parent Entity that has one or more subsidiaries (IFRS 3).

payables Person, or an entity, to whom money is owed as a consequence of the receipt of goods or services in advance of payment, known as trade payables in IASs.

percentage of completion method Method by which construction contract revenue is matched with the contract costs incurred in reaching the stage of completion, resulting in the reporting of revenue, expenses and profit which can be attributed to the proportion of work completed (IAS 11).

post-employment benefit plans Formal or informal arrangements under which an entity provides post-employment benefits for its employees (refer to IAS 19).

post-employment benefits Employee benefits (other than termination benefits) which are payable after the completion of employment (IAS 19).

potential ordinary share Financial instrument or other contract that may entitle its holder to ordinary shares (IAS 33).

pre-acquisition profits/losses Profits or losses of a subsidiary attributable to a period prior to acquisition of control by the parent.

preferred creditors Creditors entitled to full satisfaction of their claims in insolvency before other claims are met.

presentation currency Currency in which the reporting entity's financial statements are presented (IAS 21).

previous GAAP Generally accepted accounting practice that a first-time adopter used immediately before adopting IFRSs (IFRS 1).

primary financial instruments Financial instruments such as receivables, payables and equity securities that are not derivative financial instruments (IAS 32).

prior period errors Omission from, and misstatements in, the entity's financial statements for one or more periods arising from a failure to use, or misuse of, reliable information that was available when the financial statements for those periods were authorised for issue. Such errors include the effects of mathematical mistakes in applying accounting policies, oversights or misinterpretation of facts and fraud (IAS 8).

profit Residual amount that remains after expenses (including capital maintenance adjustments where appropriate) have been deducted from income (IASB framework).

profit and loss account *See* income statement.

property, plant and equipment Tangible items (non-current assets) held for use in the production or supply of goods or services for rental to others or other administrative purposes and expected to be used during more than one period (IAS 16).

proportionate consolidation – joint ventures Method of accounting whereby a venturer's share of each of the assets, liabilities, income and expenses of a jointly controlled entity is combined with similar items, or reported as a separate line, in the venturer's financial statements (IAS 31).

prospective application Applying a new accounting policy to transactions, other events and conditions occurring after the date at which the policy is changed and recognising the effect of the change in accounting estimates in the current and any future periods affected by the change (IAS 8).

provision   Liability of uncertain timing or amount (IAS 37).

purchase method   Method of consolidation that views a business combination from the perspective of the acquirer who purchases a controlling interest in the net assets of the acquiree. According to IFRS 3, all business combinations should be accounted for by applying the purchase method.

receipts and payments account   Report of cash transactions during a period. It is used in place of an income and expenditure account when it is not considered appropriate to distinguish between capital and revenue transactions or to include accruals.

receivables   Monetary amount owed by a person or organisation to the entity as a consequence of the sale of goods or services, known as trade receivables in IASs.

recognition   The process of incorporating in the balance sheet or income statement an item that meets the definition of an element of financial statements and satisfies the following criteria:
(a)   it is probable that any future economic benefit associated with the item will flow to or from the entity; and
(b)   the item has a cost or value that can be reliably measured (IASB framework).

recoverable amount   Higher of an asset's (or a cash generating unit's) fair value less costs to sell and its value in use (IAS 36).

related parties   A party is a related party of an entity if it complies with one or more of the following conditions:
(a)   directly or indirectly through intermediaries, it controls or is controlled by or is under common control with the entity (this includes parent, subsidiaries and fellow subsidiaries);
(b)   it has an interest in the entity that gives it significant influence or joint

control over the entity (this includes associates and joint ventures);
(c)   it is a member of the key management personnel of the entity or its parent;
(d)   it is a close member of the family of any individual noted above; and
(e)   it is a post-employment benefit plan for the benefit of the employees of the entity or of any entity that is itself a related party (summarised from IAS 24).

related party transaction   Transfer of resources, services or obligations between related parties, regardless of whether a price is charged (IAS 24).

reporting entity   Entity for which there are users who rely on the financial statements for information about the entity that will be useful to them for making decisions about resource allocation. A reporting entity can be a single entity or a group comprising a parent and all of its subsidiaries (refer to IASB framework and IFRS 3).

research   Original and planned investigation undertaken with the prospect of gaining new scientific or technical knowledge and understanding (IAS 38).

reserves   Retained profits or surpluses. In a not-for-profit entity they are described as accumulated funds.

residual value – intangible asset   Estimated amount which an entity would currently obtain from disposal of the asset, after deducting the expected costs of disposal, if the asset were already of the age and condition expected at the end of its useful life (IAS 38).

residual value – tangible asset   Net amount which an entity expects to obtain for an asset at the end of its useful life after deducting the expected costs of disposal (IAS 16).

resource accounting   System of accruals accounting introduced by the UK government to replace its previous cash accounting base.

restructuring   Programme that is planned and controlled by management, and materially changes either the scope of a business undertaken by an entity or the manner in which that business is conducted (IAS 37).

retention money or payments withheld Agreed proportion of a contract price withheld for a specified period after contract completion as security for fulfilment of obligations.

retirement benefit plans Arrangements whereby an entity provides benefits for its employees on or after termination of service (either in the form of annual income or as a lump sum or both) when such benefits, or the employer's contribution towards them, can be determined or estimated in advance of retirement (IAS 26).

retrospective application Applying a new accounting policy to transactions, other events and conditions as if that policy had always been applied (IAS 8).

revalued amount of an asset Fair value of an asset at the date of a revaluation, less any subsequent accumulated depreciation and accumulated impairment losses (IAS 16).

revenue Gross inflow of economic benefits during the period arising in the course of the ordinary activities of an entity when those inflows result in increases in equity, other than increases relating to contributions from equity holders (IAS 18).

revenue expenditure Expenditure on the manufacture of goods, the provision of services or on the general conduct of the entity which is charged to the income statement in the period the expenditure is incurred. This will include charges for depreciation and impairment of non-current assets as distinct from the cost of the assets. *See* capital expenditure.

reverse acquisition Acquisition where the acquirer is the entity whose equity interests have been acquired and the issuing entity is the acquiree. For example, a private entity arranges to have itself *acquired* by a smaller public entity as a means of obtaining a stock exchange listing (IFRS 3).

sale and leaseback transaction Sale of an asset to the lessor and the subsequent leasing back of the asset under an operating lease or a finance lease. The lease payments and the sale price are usually interdependent because they are negotiated as a package (IAS 17).

Sarbanes–Oxley (SOX) Act passed by US Congress in response to corporate accounting scandals "to protect investors by improving the accuracy and reliability of corporate disclosures made pursuant to the securities laws and for other purposes".

Section 404 of SOX Section 404 of the Sarbanes–Oxley Act: Management Assessment Of Internal Controls requires each annual report of an issuer to contain an internal control report, which should

(a) state the responsibility of management for establishing and maintaining an adequate internal control structure and procedures for financial reporting; and

(b) contain an assessment, as of the end of the issuer's fiscal year, of the effectiveness of the internal control structure and procedures of the issuer for financial reporting.

These internal control reports are subject to audit.

Each registered public accounting firm that prepares or issues the audit report for the issuer shall attest to, and report on, the assessment made by the management of the issuer. An attestation made under this section shall be in accordance with standards for attestation engagements issued or adopted by the Board. An attestation engagement shall not be the subject of a separate engagement.

secured creditors Creditors whose claims are wholly or partly secured on the assets of a business.

Securities and Exchange Commission (SEC) US Commission whose purpose is to protect investors and maintain the integrity of the securities markets. It does this by requiring public companies to disclose meaningful financial and other information to the public. The SEC also oversees other participants in the securities markets such as stock exchanges, broker-dealers, investment advisors, mutual funds, and public utility holding companies. The SEC is also an enforcement authority bringing four to five hundred civil actions each year against individuals and organisations which break securities laws, through insider trading, accounting fraud, or providing false or misleading information about securities or issuers.

segment reports　Reports within the financial statements that analyse revenue, profit from operations, total assets and total liabilities by reportable segments. The segments may be by business activity or geographic area (refer to IAS 14). *See* Figure 3.7.

share　Fixed identifiable unit of capital in a company (or other entity) which normally has a fixed nominal or face value, which may be quite different from its market value. *convertible share*　Non-equity share such as a preference share, carrying rights to convert into equity shares on predetermined terms. *cumulative preference shares*　Shares which entitle the holders to a fixed rate of dividend, and the right to have any

FIGURE 3.7　SEGMENT REPORT FOR THE YEAR ENDED 31 DECEMBER 2005 (REFER TO IAS 14)

	Segment A $ million	Segment B $ million	Other operations $ million	Eliminations $ million	Consolidated totals $ million
Revenue					
External sales	1,943	1,866	538		
Inter-segment sales	211	103	67	(381)	
Total revenue	2,154	1,969	605	(381)	4,347
Result					
Segment result	194	141	33	(31)	337
Unallocated corporate expenses					(52)
Profit from operations					285
Finance costs					(85)
Finance income					56
Share of profits of associates and joint ventures	127		20		147
Income tax expense					(169)
Profit for the year					234
Other information					
Segment assets	1,743	1,828	366		3,937
Investment in associates and joint ventures	652		158		810
Unallocated corporate assets					320
Consolidated total assets					5,067
Segment liabilities	(814)	(689)	(139)		(1,642)
Unallocated corporate liabilities					(1,155)
Consolidated total liabilities					(2,797)
Capital expenditure	89	99	85		273
Depreciation	40	25	15		80

arrears of dividend paid out of future profits with priority over any distribution of profits to the holders of ordinary share capital.

deferred/founders' shares Special class of shares ranking for dividend after preference and ordinary shares.

non-voting shares Shares which carry no voting rights.

ordinary shares Equity instrument that is subordinate to all other classes of equity instrument (refer to IAS 33).

participating preference shares Shares which entitle the holder to a fixed dividend and, in addition, to the right to participate in any surplus profits after payment of agreed levels of dividends to ordinary shareholders have been made.

preference shares Shares carrying a fixed rate of dividend, the holders of which, subject to the conditions of issue, have a prior claim to any profits available for distribution. Preference shareholders may also have a prior claim to the repayment of capital in the event of winding up.

redeemable shares Shares which are issued on terms which may require them to be bought back by the issuer at some future date either at the discretion of the issuer or of the holder.

share capital

authorised/nominal/registered share capital Type, class, number and amount of the shares which a company (or other entity) may issue, as empowered by its memorandum of association.

called-up share capital Amount which the entity has required shareholders to pay on the shares issued.

issued/subscribed share capital The type, class, number and amount of the shares held by shareholders.

paid-up share capital Amount which shareholders are deemed to have paid on the shares issued and called up.

uncalled share capital Amount of the nominal value of a share which is unpaid and has not been called up by the entity.

unissued share capital Amount of the share capital authorised but not yet issued.

share option Contract that gives the holder the right, but not the obligation, to subscribe to the entity's shares at a fixed or determinable price for a specific period of time (IAS 39).

share premium Excess received, either in cash or other consideration, over the nominal or face value of the shares issued.

share-based payment arrangement
An agreement between the entity and another party (including an employee) to enter into a share-based payment transaction which thereby entitles the other party to receive cash or other assets of the entity for amounts that are based on the price of the entity's shares (or other equity instruments) or to receive equity instruments in the entity (IFRS 2).

share-based payment transaction
Transaction in which the entity receives goods or services as consideration for equity instruments of the entity (including shares or share options) or acquires goods or services for amounts that are based on the price of the entity's shares (or other equity instruments) (IFRS 2).

significant influence Power to participate in the financial and operating policy decisions of an entity, but not have control over those policies. This may be gained by share ownership, statute or agreement (IAS 28).

sinking fund Money put aside periodically to settle a liability or replace an asset. The money is invested to produce a required sum at an appropriate time.

social cost Tangible and intangible costs and losses sustained by third parties or the general public as a result of economic activity, for example pollution by industrial effluent.

social responsibility accounting
Identification, measurement and reporting of the social costs and benefits resulting from economic activities.

SORP (Statement of Recommended Practice)
Supplement UK accounting standards, approved by the ASB, which recommend accounting practices for specialised industries or sectors, to allow for features or transactions undertaken in that particular industry or sector.

Standards Advisory Council (SAC)   Formal vehicle for groups and individuals to offer advice and feedback to the IASB regarding the implications of proposed Standards. The SAC has to be consulted on all major IASB projects.

statement of affairs   Statement, usually prepared by a receiver, in a prescribed form, showing the estimated financial position of a debtor or of a company (or other entity) which may be unable to meet its debts. It contains a summary of the debtor's assets and liabilities. The assets are shown at their estimated realisable values. The various classes of creditors, such as preferential, secured, partly secured and unsecured, are shown separately.

Statement of Auditing Standards (SAS)   A standard issued by the Auditing Practices Board (APB), containing prescriptions as to the basic principles and practices which members of the UK accountancy bodies are expected to follow in the course of an audit. Superseded from 2005 by International Standards on Auditing (UK and Ireland) (ISAs (UK and Ireland)), and International Standards on Quality Control (ISQC) issued by the IAASB. *See* IAASB.

statement of changes in equity   Summary of all the component changes in equity for a period (see Figure 3.8) or a summary of changes in equity other than those arising from transactions with equity holders in their capacity as equity holders (see Figure 3.9). Refer to IAS 1.

Statement of Standard Accounting Practice (SSAP)   Standard issued by the Councils of the CCAB member bodies following proposals developed by the Accounting Standards Committee. The ASC has been replaced by the ASB who adopted all the existing SSAP; those still extant in the UK are listed in Appendix 2. *See* Financial Reporting Standard.

stewardship   Responsibility of agents to act in the best interests of their principals, by keeping adequate records of transactions and by acting so as to maintain or increase both the capital and income of the principal.

stock (goods)   *See* inventories.

subordinated debt   Ranks below other debt under the terms of the agreement between the borrower and the lender.

subsidiary   Entity, including an unincorporated entity such as a partnership, that is controlled by another entity (known as the parent) (IFRS 3).

tax base (of an asset/liability)   Amount attributed to that asset or liability for tax purposes (IAS 12).

taxable profit or loss   Profit or loss for a period, determined in accordance with the rules established by the taxation authorities, upon which income (corporation) taxes are payable (or recoverable) (IAS 12).

teeming and lading   Fraud based on a continuous cycle of stealing and later replacing assets (generally cash), each theft being used in part, or in full, to repay a previous theft in order to avoid detection.

temporary difference   Difference between the carrying amount of an asset or liability in the balance sheet and its tax base. It may be either a taxable temporary difference or a deductible temporary difference (IAS 12).

temporary difference, taxable   Temporary difference that will result in taxable amounts in determining taxable profit (or loss) of future periods when the carrying amount of the asset or liability is recovered or settled (IAS 12).

termination benefits   Employee benefits payable either as a result of an entity's decision to terminate an employee's employment before the normal retirement date or an employee's decision to accept voluntary redundancy in exchange for these benefits (IAS 19).

tests of control   Tests performed to obtain audit evidence about the operating effectiveness of controls in preventing, or detecting and correcting, material misstatements at the assertion level (Glossary of terms, Auditing Standards (ISAs (UK and Ireland))).

FIGURE 3.8 STATEMENT OF CHANGES IN EQUITY FOR THE YEAR ENDED 31 DECEMBER 2005 (REFER TO IAS 1)

	Attributable to equity holders of the parent					Minority interest	Total equity
	Share capital $ million	Other reserves (see note) $ million	Translation reserve $ million	Retained earnings $ million	Total $ million	$ million	$ million
Balances at 1 January 2005	1,000	288	56	372	1,716	227	1,943
Change in accounting policy	—	—	—	(44)	(44)	(8)	(52)
Restated balances	1,000	288	56	328	1,672	219	1,891
Changes in equity for 2005							
Gain on property revaluation		110			110	20	130
Available-for-sale investments Valuation losses taken to equity		(48)			(48)	(11)	(59)
Cash flow hedges Gains taken to equity		72			72	14	86
Exchange differences on translation of foreign operations			(83)		(83)	(12)	(95)
Tax on items taken directly to or transferred from equity		(20)	15		(5)	(1)	(6)
Net income recognised directly in equity		114	(68)		46	10	56
Profit for the year		—	—	199	199	35	234
Total recognised income and expense for the year		114	(68)	199	245	45	290
Dividends				(93)	(93)	(18)	(111)
Issue of share capital	150	50			200		200
	150	164	(68)	106	352	27	379
Balances at 31 December 2005	1,150	452	(12)	434	2,024	246	2,270

Note – "Other reserves" would include the share premium and revaluation reserves which would need to be analysed separately.

timing difference Difference between the balances held on related accounts which are caused by differences in the timing of the input of common transactions, for example a direct debit will appear on the bank statement before it is entered into the bank account. Knowledge of the timing difference allows the balances on the two accounts to be reconciled.

FIGURE 3.9 STATEMENT OF RECOGNISED INCOME AND EXPENSE FOR THE YEAR ENDED 31 DECEMBER 2005 (REFER TO IAS 1)

	$ million
Gain on property revaluation	130
Available-for-sale investments	
Valuation losses taken to equity	(59)
Cash flow hedges	
Gains taken to equity	86
Exchange differences on translation of foreign operations	(95)
Tax on items taken directly to or transferred from equity	(6)
Net income recognised directly in equity	56
Profit for the year	234
Total recognised income and expense for the period	290
Attributable to:	
Equity holders of the parent	245
Minority interests	45
	290
Effects of changes in accounting policy	
Equity holders of the parent	(44)
Minority interests	(8)
	(52)

total assets   Total carrying value of all assets (non-current and current, tangible and intangible).

trade payables   *See* payables.

trade receivables   *See* receivables.

treasury shares   Shares held by an entity when it re-acquires its own equity instruments. These should be deducted from equity in the balance sheet (refer to IAS 32).

turnover/sales   *See* revenue.

Urgent Issues Task Force (UITF)   Committee of the ASB whose aim is to assist the ASB in areas where unsatisfactory or conflicting interpretations of an accounting standard have developed, or seem likely to develop. Abstracts published by the UITF have the same legal status as accounting standards.

useful life (assets)   Estimated period over which an asset is expected to be available for use by an entity or the number of production or similar units expected to be obtained from the asset by the entity (IAS 16).

user groups   Different interest groups who may make use of publicly available financial statements. Lenders, employees, investors and competitors may be classed as separate user groups.

value in use   Present value of the estimated future cash flows expected to arise from the continuing use of an asset (or cash generating unit) and from its disposal at the end of its useful life (IFRS 5).

venturer   Party to a joint venture that has joint control over that joint venture (IAS 31).

wasting asset   Non-current asset which is consumed or exhausted in the process of earning income, for example a mine or quarry.

window-dressing   Creative accounting practice in which changes in short-term funding have the effect of disguising or improving the reported liquidity position of the reporting entity.

withholding tax   Tax on dividends or other income that is deducted by the payer of the income and paid to the taxation authorities on behalf of the recipient.

working capital   Capital available for conducting the day-to-day operations of an entity, normally the excess of current assets over current liabilities.

Corporate Finance and Treasury

ad valorem (duty)   Duty based on the value of a product or service.

adjusted present value (APV)   Net present value of an asset that also takes account of any financing side effects.

Alternative Investment Market (AIM) Securities market designed primarily for small companies, regulated by the UK stock exchange but with less demanding rules than apply to the stock exchange official list of companies.

annual equivalent rate (AER)   Notional annual rate which is equivalent to another set of rates that may be paid other than annually.

annuity   Fixed periodic payment which continues either for a specified time, or until the occurrence of a specified event. *See* perpetuity.

arbitrage   Simultaneous purchase and sale of a security in different markets with the aim of making a risk-free profit through the exploitation of any price difference between the markets.

arrangement fees   *See* issue costs.

articles of association   Document which, with the memorandum of association, provides the legal constitution of a company. The articles of association define the rules and regulations governing the management of the affairs of the company, the rights of the members (shareholders), and the duties and powers of the directors. *See* memorandum of association.

back-to-back loan   Form of financing whereby money borrowed in one country, or currency is covered by lending an equivalent amount in another.

BACS   (Formerly the Bankers Automated Clearing Services). UK electronic bulk clearing system generally used by banks and building societies for low-value and/or repetitive items such as standing orders, direct debits and automated credits such as salary payments.

balancing allowance/charge   Relief for tax purposes of capital expenditure, or the claw back of relief already given, administered in the year in which a real asset is disposed of or an entity ceases to exist.

bank charge   Amount charged by a bank to its customers for services provided, for example for servicing customer accounts or arranging foreign currency transactions or letters of credit, but excluding interest.

bank overdraft   Borrowings from a bank on current account, normally repayable on demand. The maximum permissible overdraft is normally agreed with the bank prior to the facility being made available, and interest, calculated on a daily basis, is charged on the amount borrowed, and not on the agreed maximum borrowing facility.

bank reconciliation   Detailed statement reconciling, at a given date, the cash balance in an entity's cash book with that reported in a bank statement. An example is given below:

Bank Reconciliation Statement

Cash book balance

	$	$
Cash book balance o/d		(1,205)
Bank charges not in cash book	(110)	
Dividends collected by the bank, not in cash book	113	3
Updated cash book balance*		**(1,202)**
Cheques drawn, not presented to bank	4,363	
Cheques received, not yet credited by bank	(1,061)	3,302
Bank statement balance		**2,100**

* The balance sheet will show a bank overdraft of $1,202, which is the true position at the date of the reconciliation, after corrections by journal entry.

bankruptcy Legal status of an individual against whom an adjudication order has been made by the court primarily because of inability to meet financial liabilities.

bear market Securities market experiencing a prolonged widespread decline in prices. *See* bull market.

bearer bond Negotiable bond (or security) whose ownership is not registered by the issuer, but is presumed to lie with whoever has physical possession of the bond.

beta factor Measure of systematic risk of a security relative to the market portfolio. If a security were to rise or fall at double the market rate, it would have a beta factor of 2.0. Conversely, if the security price moved at half the market rate, the beta factor would be 0.5. *See* risk, market/systematic.

bid-ask spread Difference between the buying and selling prices of a traded commodity or a financial instrument. Also known as *bid-offer spread*.

bill of lading Document prepared by a consignor by which a carrier acknowledges the receipt of goods and which serves as a document of title to the goods consigned.

bill payable Bill of exchange or promissory note payable.

bill receivable Bill of exchange or promissory note receivable.

Black-Scholes method (share options) Equation developed by F. Black and M. Scholes to value a European-style call option that uses the share price, the exercise price, the risk-free interest rate, the time to maturity and the standard deviation of the share return. A European option can be exercised only on the expiration date. *See* European-style option (option).

blue chip Description of an equity or company which is of the highest quality, and in which an investment would be regarded as low risk with regard to both dividend payments and capital values.

bond Debt instrument, normally offering a fixed rate of interest (coupon) over a fixed period of time, and with a fixed redemption value (par).

bonus/scrip issue Capitalisation of the reserves of an entity by the issue of additional shares to existing shareholders in proportion to their holdings. Such shares are normally fully paid-up with no cash called for from the shareholders. *See* rights issue.

borrowing costs Interest and other costs incurred by an entity in connection with the borrowing of funds. They may include:
(a) interest on bank overdrafts and borrowings;
(b) amortisation of discounts or premiums related to borrowings;
(c) amortisation of ancillary costs incurred in connection with the arrangement of borrowings;
(d) finance charges in respect to finance leases; and
(e) exchange differences arising from foreign currency borrowings to the extent they are regarded as an adjustment to interest costs (IAS 23).

bull market Securities market experiencing prolonged widespread price increases. *See* bear market.

business angels Wealthy individuals prepared to invest in a start-up, early stage or developing firm. Often, they have managerial and/or technical experience to offer to the management team as well as debt and equity finance.

call Request made to the holders of partly paid-up share capital for the payment of a predetermined sum due on the share capital, under the terms of the original subscription agreement. Failure on the part of the shareholder to pay a call may result in the forfeiture of the relevant holding of partly paid shares.

call option Option to buy a specified underlying asset at a specified exercise price on, or before, a specified exercise date. *See* exercise price, option, put option.

capital allowance   Relief from income tax or corporation tax on capital expenditure on eligible assets.

capital asset pricing model (CAPM)   Theory which predicts that the expected risk premium for an individual stock will be proportional to its beta, such that:

(Expected risk premium on a stock = beta × expected risk premium in the market.)

Risk premium is defined as the expected incremental return for making a risky investment rather than a safe one.

capital budgeting   Process concerned with decision-making in respect of the choice of specific investment projects and the total amount of capital expenditure to commit.

capital instrument   All instruments that are issued by reporting entities as a means of raising finance, including shares, debentures, loans and debt instruments, options and warrants that give the holder the right to subscribe for or obtain capital instruments. In the case of consolidated financial statements the term includes capital instruments issued by subsidiaries except those that are held by another member of the group included in the consolidation (FRS 4).

capital investment appraisal   Application of a set of methodologies (generally based on the discounting of projected cash flows) whose purpose is to give guidance to managers with respect to decisions as to how best to commit long-term investment funds. *See* discounted cash flow.

capital rationing   Restriction on an entity's ability to invest capital funds, caused by an internal budget ceiling being imposed on such expenditure by management (soft capital rationing), or by external limitations being applied to the company, as when additional borrowed funds cannot be obtained (hard capital rationing).

capital structure   Relative proportions of equity capital and debt capital within an entity's balance sheet.

cash management models   Sophisticated cash flow forecasting models which assist management in determining how to balance the cash needs of an entity. Cash management models can help: to optimise cash balances; to manage customer, supplier, investor and company needs; the determine whether to invest or buy back shares; and to decide what is the optimum of financing working captial.

certainty equivalent method   Approach to dealing with risk in a capital budgeting context. It involves expressing risky future cash flows in terms of the certain cash flow which would be considered, by the decision maker, as their equivalent, that is the decision maker would be indifferent between the risky amount and the (lower) riskless amount considered to be its equivalent.

certificate of deposit   Negotiable instrument which provides evidence of a fixed-term deposit with a bank. Maturity is normally within 90 days, but can be longer.

CHAPS   Clearing House Automated Payment System. UK method for the rapid electronic transfer of funds between participating banks on behalf of large commercial customers, where transfers tend to be of significant value.

chartered entity   Organisation formed by the grant of a Royal Charter (in the UK). The charter authorises the entity to operate and states the powers specifically granted.

collateral   Security, in the form of a claim over assets, generally given for borrowed funds over the period of a loan.

commercial paper   Unsecured short-term loan notes issued by companies, and generally maturing within a period of up to one year.

commodity pricing   Pricing a product or service on the basis that it is undifferentiated from all competitive offerings, and cannot therefore command any price premium above the base market price.

company limited by guarantee   Company in which each member undertakes to contribute (to the limit of the guarantee), on a winding up, towards payment of the liabilities of the company.

company limited by shares/joint stock company/limited liability company
Company in which the liability of members for the company's debts is limited to the value of the shares taken up by them. *See* private company and public company.

company/corporation Legal entity, whose life is independent of that of its members. In the UK, companies or corporations are predominantly formed through registration under the UK Companies Act 1985.

compound interest Interest which is calculated over successive periods based on the principal plus accrued interest. *See* simple interest. The future value of an investment, over whose period interest is compounded, can be found by using the following formula:

$$S = X(1 + r)^n$$

where:
S = Future value in year n
X = Initial investment, principal or value at
   year 0
r = Annual rate of return expressed as a
   decimal fraction
n = Number of years

Example:
Investment of $400 (X)
Time period of 4 years (n)
Annual interest is 8% (r)

$$S = \$400(1 + 0.08)^4 = \$544.20$$

conglomerate Entity comprising a number of dissimilar businesses.

consol Certain irredeemable UK government stocks carrying fixed coupons. Sometimes used as a general term for an undated or irredeemable bond.

consortium Association of several entities with a view to carrying out a joint venture. *See* joint venture.

cost of capital Minimum acceptable return on an investment, generally computed as a discount rate for use in investment appraisal exercises. The computation of the optimal cost of capital can be complex, and many ways of determining this opportunity cost have been suggested. *See* weighted average cost of capital.

countertrade Form of trading activity based on other than an arm's-length goods for cash exchange. Types of countertrade include:
barter Direct exchange of goods and services between two parties without the use of money.
counterpurchase Trading agreement in which the primary contract vendor agrees to make purchases of an agreed percentage of the primary contract value, from the primary contract purchaser, through a linked counterpurchase contract.
offsets Trading agreement in which the purchaser becomes involved in the production process, often acquiring technology supplied by the vendor.

coupon Interest payable on a bond expressed as a percentage of the nominal value.

credit scoring Assessment of the creditworthiness of an individual or company by rating numerically a number of both financial and non-financial aspects of the target's present position and previous performance.

cum "With", as in *cum dividend*, where security purchases include rights to the next dividend payment, and *cum rights*, where shares are traded with rights, such as to a scrip issue, attached.

debt capacity Extent to which an entity can support and/or obtain loan finance.

deep discount bond Bond offered at a large discount on the face value of the debt so that a significant proportion of the return to the investor comes by way of a capital gain on redemption, rather than through interest payments.

discount rate (capital investment appraisal)
Percentage rate used to discount future cash flows generated by a capital project.

discounted cash flow (DCF)   Discounting of the projected net cash flows of a capital project to ascertain its return or present value. The methods commonly used are:

discounted payback   The discount rate is used to calculate the present values of periodic cash flows with a payback period then being calculated.

net present value (NPV)   The discount rate is chosen and the present value is expressed as a sum of money.

yield, or internal rate of return (IRR)   The calculation determines the return in the form of a percentage.

   See capital investment appraisal, net present value, internal rate of return and discounted payback.

discounted payback   Capital investment method with the aim of determining the period of time required to recover initial cash outflow when net cash inflows are discounted at the opportunity cost of capital. Also *see* payback and discounted cash flow.

divestment   Disposal of part of its activities by an entity.

dividend growth model   Way of assessing the value of shares by capitalising future dividends that grow at a constant rate.

dividend yield

$$\frac{\text{Dividend per share net of any taxes deducted at source} \times 100}{\text{Market price per share}}$$

   Post-tax dividend return on market value offered by the shares shown as a percentage.

documentary credit   Arrangement, used in the finance of international transactions, whereby a bank undertakes to make a payment to a third party on behalf of a customer.

double taxation agreement   Agreement between two countries intended to avoid the double taxation of income which would otherwise be subject to taxation in both.

earnings yield

$$\frac{\text{Earnings per share} \times 100}{\text{Market price of a share}}$$

   As a percentage, indicates the total amount earned in respect of each equity share in issue, in relation to the market price of the share. The earnings yield computation can also be based on the aggregate earnings and the market value of the equity capital.

earn-out arrangement   Procedure whereby owners/managers selling an entity receive a portion of their consideration linked to the financial performance of the business during a specified period after the sale. The arrangement gives a measure of security to the new owners, who pass some of the financial risk associated with the purchase of a new enterprise to the sellers.

economic exposure   Risk that a company's future cash flows will vary as a result of changes in exchange rates.

economic value added (EVA™)   Profit less a charge for capital employed in the period. Accounting profit may be adjusted, for example, for the treatment of goodwill and research and development expenditure, before economic value added is calculated (Stern Stewart & Co).

economies of scale   Reductions in unit average costs caused by increasing the scale of production.

economies of scope   Reduction in unit average costs caused by the simultaneous production of a number of related products, permitting benefits such as the sharing of joint costs over a larger volume than would otherwise be possible.

efficient markets hypothesis   Hypothesis that the stock market responds immediately to all available information with the effect that an individual investor cannot, in the long run, expect to obtain greater than average returns from a diversified portfolio of shares. There are three forms:

weak form   Market in which security prices instantaneously reflect all information on past price and volume changes in the market.

semi-strong form   Market in which security prices reflect all publicly available information.

strong form   Market in which security prices reflect instantaneously all information available to investors whether publicly available or otherwise.

electronic funds transfer   System used by the banking sector for the movement of funds between accounts and for the provision of services to the customer.

eurobond   Bond sold outside the jurisdiction of the country in whose currency the bond is denominated.

eurodollars   US dollars deposited with, or borrowed from, a bank outside the US.

ex   "Without", as in *ex dividend*, where security purchases do not include rights to the next dividend payment, and *ex rights*, where rights attaching to share ownership, such as a scrip issue, are not transferred to a new purchaser.

exchange controls   Restrictions in the convertibility of a currency, generally enforced by central banks on the instruction of national governments.

exchange difference   Difference (profit or loss) resulting from translating a given number of units of one currency into another currency at different exchange rates (IAS 21).

exchange rate   Rate at which a national currency exchanges for other national currencies, being set by the interaction of demand and supply of the various currencies in the foreign exchange market (floating exchange rate), or by government intervention in order to maintain a constant rate of exchange (fixed exchange rate).

closing rate   Spot transactions ruling at the balance sheet date, being the mean of the buying and selling rates at the close of business on the day for which the rate is to be ascertained.

forward exchange rate   Set for the exchange of currencies at some future date.

spot exchange rate   Set for the immediate delivery of a currency.

exercise price   The price at which an option to purchase or to sell shares or other items (*call option* or *put option*) may be exercised. *See* call option, put option.

expected value/payoff   Financial forecast of the outcome of a course of action multiplied by the probability of achieving that outcome. The probability is expressed as a value ranging from 0 to 1.

externalities   Benefits or costs arising from an activity which does not accrue to the entity or person carrying on the activity.

factoring   Sale of debts to a third party (the factor) at a discount in return for prompt cash. A factoring service may be *with recourse*, in which case the supplier takes the risk of the debt not being paid, or *without recourse* when the factor takes the risk. *See* invoice discounting.

financial asset   Any asset that is:
(a)   cash;
(b)   an equity instrument of another entity;
(c)   a contractual right: (i) to receive cash or another financial asset from another entity, or (ii) to exchange financial assets or financial liabilities with another entity under conditions that are potentially favourably to the entity; or
(d)   a contract that will or may be settled in the entity's own equity instruments and is: (i) a non-derivative for which the entity is or may be obliged to receive a variable number of the entity's own equity instruments, or (ii) a derivative that will or may be settled other than by the exchange of a fixed amount of cash or other financial asset for a fixed number of the entity's own equity instruments (IAS 32).

financial control   Control of the performance of an entity by setting a range of financial targets and the monitoring of actual performance towards these targets.

financial instrument　Any contract that gives rise to a financial asset of one entity and a financial liability of another entity (IAS 32).

financial instrument, derivative　Financial instrument or other contract with all three of the following characteristics:
(a) its value changes in response to the change in a specified interest rate, financial instrument price, commodity price, foreign exchange rate, index of prices or rates, credit rating or credit index, or other variable, provided in the case of a non-financial variable that the variable is not specific to a party to the contract (sometimes called the *underlying*);
(b) it requires no initial net investment or an initial net investment that is smaller than would be required for other types of contracts that would be expected to have a similar response to changes in market forces; and
(c) it is settled at a future date (IAS 39).

financial leverage/gearing　Amount of debt, in relation to equity, in the capital structure of an entity or debt interest in relation to profit. An entity with no gearing has no debt.

financial liability　Any liability that is:
(a) a contractual obligation: (i) to deliver cash or another financial asset to another entity; or (ii) to exchange financial assets or financial liabilities with another entity under conditions that are potentially unfavourable to the entity; or
(b) a contract that will or may be settled in the entity's own equity instruments and is: (i) a non-derivative for which the entity is or may be obliged to deliver a variable number of the entity's own equity instruments; or (ii) a derivative that may or will be settled other than by the exchange of a fixed amount of cash or another financial asset for a fixed amount of the entity's own equity instruments (IAS 32).

financial management　Management of all the processes associated with the efficient acquisition and deployment of both short- and long-term financial resources.

Financial Services Authority (FSA)　An independent body that regulates the financial services industry in the UK, with powers in rule-making, investigation and enforcement. Its broad task is to achieve a marketplace that is run in an efficient, orderly and fair manner whilst ensuring that consumers are properly informed and appropriately protected.

floating rate financial assets and financial liabilities　Financial assets and financial liabilities that attract an interest charge and have their interest rate reset at least once a year. For the purpose of the FRS, financial assets and financial liabilities that have their interest rate reset less frequently than once a year are to be treated as fixed rate financial assets and financial liabilities (FRS 13).

foreign direct investment (FDI)　Establishment of new overseas facilities or the expansion of existing overseas facilities by an investor. FDI may be *inward* (domestic investment by overseas companies) or *outward* (overseas investment by domestic companies).

forfaiting　Purchase of financial instruments such as bills of exchange or letters of credit on a non-recourse basis by a forfaiter, who deducts interest (in the form of a discount) at an agreed rate for the period covered by the notes. The forfaiter assumes the responsibility for claiming the debt from the importer (buyer) who initially accepted the financial instrument drawn by the seller of the goods. Traditionally, forfaiting is fixed-rate, medium-term (one- to five-year) finance. *See* invoice discounting.

forward contract　Agreement to exchange different currencies at a specified future date and at a specified rate. The difference between the specified rate and the spot rate ruling on the date the contract was entered into is the discount or premium on the forward contract (SSAP 20).

free cash flow Cash flow from operations after deducting interest, tax, preference dividends and ongoing capital expenditure, but excluding capital expenditure associated with strategic acquisitions and/or disposals and ordinary share dividends.

functional currency Currency of the primary economic environment in which the entity operates (IAS 21).

fundamental analysis Analysis of external and internal influences that directly affect the operations of a company with a view to assisting in investment decisions. Information accessed might include fiscal/monetary policy, financial statements, industry trends and competitor analysis. *See* technical analysis.

futures contract Contract relating to currencies, interest rates, commodities or shares that obliges the buyer (seller) to purchase (sell) the specified quantity of the item represented in the contract at a predetermined price at the expiration of the contract. Unlike forward contracts, which are entered into privately, futures contracts are traded on organised exchanges, carry standard terms and conditions, have specific maturities and are subject to rules concerning margin requirements.

futures market Exchange-traded market for the purchase or sale of a standard quantity of an underlying item such as currencies, commodities or shares for settlement at a future date at an agreed price.

hedge Transaction to reduce or eliminate an exposure to risk.

hedge funds Generally actively managed with greater freedom than conventional mutual funds to borrow heavily and use high-risk investment strategies, such as selling short and using derivatives, to make absolute returns even in falling markets.

hire purchase contract A contract for the hire of an asset that contains a provision giving the hirer an option to acquire title to the asset upon the fulfilment of agreed conditions (IAS 17).

hurdle rate Rate of return which a capital investment proposal must achieve if it is to be accepted. Set by reference to the cost of capital, the hurdle rate may be increased above the basic cost of capital to allow for different levels of risk.

incremental yield Measure used in capital investment appraisal where a choice lies between two projects. A rate of return is calculated for the difference between the cash flows of the projects.

inflation General increase in the price level over time measured by a retail price index.

insolvency Inability of a debtor to pay debts when they fall due.

interest rate parity theory Method of predicting foreign exchange rates based on the hypothesis that the difference between the interest rates in two countries should offset the difference between the spot rates and the forward foreign exchange rates over the same period.

interest yield Annual rate of interest earned on a security, excluding the effect of any increase in price to maturity.

inter-firm comparison Systematic and detailed comparison of the performance of different entities generally operating in a common industry. Entities participating in such a scheme normally provide standardised, and therefore comparable, information to the scheme administrator, who then distributes to participating members only the information supplied by participants. Normally the information distributed is in the form of ratios, or in a format which prevents the identity of individual scheme members from being identified.

internal rate of return (IRR) Annual percentage return achieved by a project, at which the sum of the discounted cash inflows over the life of the project is equal to the sum of the discounted cash outflows. *See* discounted cash flow.

invoice discounting Sale of debts to a third party at a discount in return for prompt cash. The administration is managed in such a way that the debtor is generally unaware of the discounter's involvement and continues to pay the supplier. *See* factoring and forfaiting.

issue costs   The costs that are incurred directly in connection with the issue of a capital instrument, that is those costs which would have not been incurred if the specific instrument in question had not been issued (FRS 4).

junk bond   High-yielding bond issued on low-grade security. The issue of junk bonds has most commonly been linked with takeover activity. Bonds may also assume junk status when the issuer is at risk of insolvency.

liquidation   Winding up of a company, in which the assets are sold, liabilities settled as far as possible and any remaining cash returned to the members. Liquidation may be voluntary or compulsory.

liquidity   Availability of sufficient funds to meet financial commitments as they fall due (refer to IAS 30).

London interbank offered rate (LIBOR)   Rate of interest at which banks borrow funds in the London interbank market for a given maturity, normally ranging between overnight and one year.

London International Financial Futures and Options Exchange (LIFFE)   The combined French, Belgian, Portuguese and Dutch exchange operator. Now known as Euronext.liffe since its takeover in 2002 by Euronext.

management buy-in (MBI)   New team of managers makes an offer to an entity to buy the whole entity, a subsidiary or a section of it, with the intention of taking over the entity.

management buy-out (MBO)   Purchase of a business from its existing owners by members of the management team, generally in association with a financing institution. Where a large proportion of the new finance required to purchase the business is raised by external borrowing, the buy-out is described as *leveraged*.

market risk premium   Difference between the expected rate of return on a market portfolio and the risk-free rate of return over the same period. *See* risk, market/systematic.

market value added (MVA)   The difference between a company's market value (derived from the share price) and its economic book value (the amount of capital that shareholders and debt holders have committed to the firm throughout its existence, including any retained earnings).

memorandum of association   Document which, with the articles of association, provides the legal constitution of a company. The memorandum states the name and registered office of the company. It also defines its powers and objects and usually states that the liability of its members is limited. *See* articles of association.

merger   Business combination that results in the creation of a new reporting entity formed from the combining parties, in which the shareholders of the combining entities come together in a partnership for the mutual sharing of the risks and benefits of the combined entity, and in which no party to the combination in substance obtains control over any other, or is otherwise seen to be dominant, whether by virtue of the proportion of its shareholders' rights in the combined entity, the influence of its directors or otherwise (FRS 6). However, IFRS 3 *Business Combinations* requires all business combinations to be accounted for by applying the purchase method which necessitates the identification of a purchaser and seller and so effectively rules out the possibility of using merger accounting as opposed to acquisition accounting.

  A demerger takes place when the merger process is reversed, and separate entities emerge from the merged body.

money market   Short-term wholesale market for securities usually maturing in less than one year such as certificates of deposit, treasury bills and commercial paper.

moral hazard   Risk that the existence of a contract will cause behavioural changes in one or both parties to the contract. For example, insuring an asset causes its owner to take less care of it.

negotiable instrument Document of title which can be freely traded such as a bill of exchange or other certificate of debt.

net present value (NPV) Difference between the sum of the projected discounted cash inflows and outflows attributable to a capital investment or other long-term project. *See* discounted cash flow.

nominal interest rate Interest rate expressed in money terms.

nominee holding Shareholding in a company registered in the name of an agent, instead of that of the owner.

offer for sale An invitation to the public to apply for shares in a company based on information contained in a prospectus.

option Right of an option holder to buy or sell a specific asset on predetermined terms on, or before, a future date.

European-style option Option that can be exercised only at the expiration date.

American-style option Option that can be exercised at any time prior to expiration. *See* call option, put option.

over the counter (OTC) market Securities trading carried on outside regulated exchanges. Allows tailor-made transactions.

over/undercapitalisation Surplus or deficiency of permanent capital in relation to the current level of activity of a business.

overtrading The condition of an entity's which enters into commitments in excess of its available short-term resources. This can arise even if an entity is trading profitably, and is typically caused by financing strains imposed by a lengthy operating cycle or production cycle. Undercapitalised new businesses are prone to suffer from overtrading.

par Nominal value of a bond, being the price denominated for the purpose of setting the interest rate (coupon) payable.

partnership Relationship which exists between persons carrying on business in common with a view to profit (UK Partnership Act 1890). The liability of the individual partners is unlimited unless the partnership agreement provides for any limitation.

The UK Limited Partnership Act 1907 allows a partnership to contain one or more partners with limited liability so long as there is at least one partner with unlimited liability.

A partnership consists of not more than twenty persons, except in certain cases, for example practising solicitors, professional accountants and members of the Stock Exchange, where this figure may be exceeded. Other limited partnerships may exist.

partnership, limited liability (LLP) Legal entity that combines the organisational flexibility and tax status of a partnership with limited liability for its members. This limited liability is possible because an LLP is a legal person separate from its members (UK Limited Liability Partnerships Act 2000).

payback Time required for the cash inflows from a capital investment project to equal the cash outflows. *See* discounted payback.

perpetuity Periodic payment continuing for a limitless period. *See* annuity.

placing Method of raising share capital in which there is no public issue of shares, the shares being issued, rather, in a small number of large 'blocks', to persons or institutions who have previously agreed to purchase the shares at a predetermined price. *See* private placement.

present value Cash equivalent now of a sum receivable or payable at a future date. *See* Figure 4.1.

private company Company which has not been registered as a public company under the UK Companies Act 1985. The major practical distinction between a private and public company is that the former may not offer its securities to the public. *See* public company.

FIGURE 4.1 PRESENT VALUE TABLES

Present value table
Present value of 1, i.e. $(1 + r)^{-n}$ where r = discount rate, n = number of periods until payment.

Periods (n)	1%	2%	3%	4%	Discount rates (r) 5%	6%	7%	8%	9%	10%
1	0.990	0.980	0.971	0.962	0.952	0.943	0.935	0.926	0.917	0.909
2	0.980	0.961	0.943	0.925	0.907	0.890	0.873	0.857	0.842	0.826
3	0.971	0.942	0.915	0.889	0.864	0.840	0.816	0.794	0.772	0.751
4	0.961	0.924	0.888	0.855	0.823	0.792	0.763	0.735	0.708	0.683
5	0.951	0.906	0.863	0.822	0.784	0.747	0.713	0.681	0.650	0.621
6	0.942	0.888	0.837	0.790	0.746	0.705	0.666	0.630	0.596	0.564
7	0.933	0.871	0.813	0.760	0.711	0.665	0.623	0.583	0.547	0.513
8	0.923	0.853	0.789	0.731	0.677	0.627	0.582	0.540	0.502	0.467
9	0.914	0.837	0.766	0.703	0.645	0.592	0.544	0.500	0.460	0.424
10	0.905	0.820	0.744	0.676	0.614	0.558	0.508	0.463	0.422	0.386
11	0.896	0.804	0.722	0.650	0.585	0.527	0.475	0.429	0.388	0.350
12	0.887	0.788	0.702	0.625	0.557	0.497	0.444	0.397	0.356	0.319
13	0.879	0.773	0.681	0.601	0.530	0.469	0.415	0.368	0.326	0.290
14	0.870	0.758	0.661	0.577	0.505	0.442	0.388	0.340	0.299	0.263
15	0.861	0.743	0.642	0.555	0.481	0.417	0.362	0.315	0.275	0.239

Cumulative present value of $1
This table shows the present value of $1 per annum. Receivable or payable at the end of each year for n years.

Present (n)	1%	2%	3%	4%	Interest rates (r) 5%	6%	7%	8%	9%	10%
1	0.990	0.980	0.971	0.962	0.952	0.943	0.935	0.926	0.917	0.909
2	1.970	1.942	1.913	1.886	1.859	1.833	1.808	1.783	1.759	1.736
3	2.941	2.884	2.829	2.775	2.723	2.673	2.624	2.577	2.531	2.487
4	3.902	3.808	3.717	3.630	3.546	3.465	3.387	3.312	3.240	3.170
5	4.853	4.713	4.580	4.452	4.329	4.212	4.100	3.993	3.890	3.791
6	5.795	5.601	5.417	5.242	5.076	4.917	4.767	4.623	4.486	4.355
7	6.727	6.472	6.230	6.002	5.786	5.582	5.389	5.206	5.033	4.868
8	7.652	7.325	7.020	6.733	6.463	6.210	5.971	5.747	5.535	5.335
9	8.566	8.162	7.786	7.435	7.108	6.802	6.515	6.247	5.995	5.759
10	9.471	8.983	8.530	8.111	7.722	7.360	7.024	6.710	6.418	6.145
11	10.368	9.787	9.253	8.760	8.306	7.887	7.499	7.139	6.805	6.495
12	11.255	10.575	9.954	9.385	8.863	8.384	7.943	7.536	7.161	6.814
13	12.134	11.348	10.635	9.986	9.394	8.853	8.358	7.904	7.487	7.103
14	13.004	12.106	11.296	10.563	9.899	9.295	8.745	8.244	7.786	7.367
15	13.865	12.849	11.938	11.118	10.38	9.712	9.108	8.559	8.061	7.606

private finance initiative (PFI) UK Policy designed to harness private sector management and expertise in the delivery of public services. Under PFI, the public sector does not buy assets, it buys the asset-based services it requires, on contract, from the private sector, the latter having the responsibility for deciding how to supply these services, the investment required to support the services and how to achieve the required standards.

private placement Issue of shares sold to one or to a limited number of investors, rather than being offered to the market. *See* placing.

profit sharing Allocation of a proportion of company profit to stakeholders, for example employees, by an issue of shares or other means.

project management Integration of all aspects of a project, ensuring that the proper knowledge and resources are available when and where needed, and above all to ensure that the expected outcome is produced in a timely, cost-effective manner. The primary function of a project manager is to manage the trade-offs between performance, timeliness and cost.

prospectus   Description of a company's operations, financial background, prospects and the detailed terms and conditions relating to an offer for sale or placing of its shares by notice, circular, advertisement or any form of invitation which offers securities to the public.

public company   UK Company limited by shares or by guarantee, with a share capital, whose memorandum of association states that it is public and that it has complied with the registration procedures for such a company.

A public company is distinguished from a private company in the following ways:
- a minimum issued share capital of £50,000;
- public limited company or plc at the end of the name;
- public company clause in the memorandum; and
- freedom to offer securities to the public. *See* private company.

purchasing power parity   Theory stating that the exchange rate between two currencies is in equilibrium when the purchasing power of currency is the same in each country. If a basket of goods costs £100 in the UK and $150 for an equivalent in the US, for equilibrium to exist, the exchange rate would be expected to be £1 = $1.50. If this were not the case, *arbitrage* would be expected to take place until equilibrium was restored.

put option   Option to sell a specified underlying asset at a specified exercise price on, or before, a specified exercise date. *See* call option and option.

quasi-subsidiary   Company, trust, partnership or other vehicle that, though not fulfilling the definition of a subsidiary,

is directly or indirectly controlled by the reporting entity and gives rise to benefits for that entity that are in substance no different from those that would arise were the vehicle a subsidiary. Typically used in the UK (refer to FRS 5).

real interest rate   Interest rate approximately calculated by adjusting the nominal or money interest rate for the rate of inflation. It, therefore, represents the rate of interest in the absence of inflation.

$$r = ((1 + n)/(1 + i)) - 1\%$$

where,
r = real rate of interest
n = nominal rate of interest
i = rate of inflation

real option   Right, but not the obligation, to take different courses of action (for example defer, abandon and expand) with respect to real assets (for example an oil well, a new product or an acquisition) as opposed to an option on financial securities or commodities.

receivership   Under the control of a receiver, who is appointed by secured creditors or by the court to take control of company property. The most usual reason for the appointment of a receiver is the failure of a company to pay principal sums or interest due to debenture holders whose debt is secured by fixed or floating charges over the assets of the company.

recourse   Source of redress should a debt be dishonoured at maturity.

redemption   Repayment of the principal amount (for example, a bond) at the date of maturity.

redemption yield   Rate of interest at which the total of the discounted values of any future payments of interest and capital is equal to the current price of a security.

regulated price   Selling price set within guidelines laid down by a regulatory authority, normally governmental.

revolving credit   A credit facility which allows the borrower, within an overall credit limit and for a set period, to borrow or repay debt as required.

rights issue   Raising of new capital by giving existing shareholders the right to subscribe to new shares in proportion to their current holdings. These shares are usually issued at a discount to market price. A shareholder not wishing to take up a rights issue may sell the rights. *See* bonus/scrip issue.

scrip dividend   Dividend paid by the issue of additional company shares, rather than by cash.

securitisation   Conversion of financial or physical assets into financial instruments that can be traded, often through the use of special purpose vehicles.

seed money   Equity investment into a new business by venture capitalists in order to finance the period of start-up and/or early trading. The provision of the (high-risk) seed money enables the new business to become established, such that it can ultimately raise equity on an established exchange, at which time venture capitalists would expect to realise their holding of shares, in so doing hoping to make a significant capital gain.

service level agreement   Contract between service provider and customer which specifies in detail the level of service to be provided over the contract period (for example quality, frequency, flexibility, charges) as well as the procedures to be implemented in the case of default.

shareholder value   Total return to the shareholders in terms of both dividends and share price growth, calculated as the present value of future free cash flows of the business discounted at the weighted average cost of the capital of the business less the market value of its debt.

short-termism   Bias towards paying particular attention to short-term performance with a corresponding relative disregard to the long-run.

simple interest   Interest which is calculated over successive periods based only on the principal. *See* compound interest.

small and medium-sized enterprise (SME) Classification used by policy-makers to specify which categories of enterprise are affected by regulation (for example the requirement for statutory audit) or are eligible for assistance. *See* Figure 4.2.

FIGURE 4.2 CLASSIFICATION FOR SMALL AND MEDIUM-SIZED ENTERPRISES (SMEs)

SMEs	Department of Trade & Industry (UK)	European Commission	World Bank Group
Medium			
staff	<250	<250	<300
turnover	<£22.8m	<€50m	total annual reserves < US$15m
balance sheet	<£11.4m	<€43m	total assets US$15m
Small			
staff	<50	<50	<50
turnover	<£5.6m	<€10m	total annual reserves < US$3m
balance sheet	<£2.8m	<€10m	total assets < US$3m
Micro			
staff	n/a	<10	<10
turnover	n/a	<€2m	total annual reserves < US$100,000
balance sheet	n/a	<€2m	total assets < US$100,000

(< less than)

sole trader Person carrying on business with total legal responsibility for his/her actions neither in partnership nor as a company.

spot rate Current rate (typically of interest or currency exchange) available in the market today.

statutory body Entity formed by a UK Act of the Parliament.

stock exchange Registered market in securities.

strategic financial management Identification of the possible strategies capable of maximising an entity's net present value, the allocation of scarce capital resources among the competing opportunities and the implementation and monitoring of the chosen strategy so as to achieve stated objectives.

strategic investment appraisal Method of investment appraisal which allows the inclusion of both financial and non-financial factors. Project benefits are appraised in terms of their contribution to the strategies of the organisation either by their financial contribution or, for non-financial benefits, by the use of index numbers or other means. *See* investment appraisal.

swap Contract to exchange payments of some sort in the future.

takeover Acquisition by a company of a controlling interest in the voting share capital of another company, usually achieved by the purchase of a majority of the voting shares.

tax avoidance Organisation of a taxpayer's affairs so that the minimum tax liability is incurred. Tax avoidance involves making the maximum use of all legal means of minimising liability to taxation.

tax evasion Minimisation of tax liability by illegal means, such as by the under-declaration of income.

tax shield Reduction in tax payable due to the use of tax-allowable deductions against taxable income. It is measured by the discounted value of future tax savings generated by the available tax reliefs.

technical analysis Analysis of past movements in the prices of, amongst other things, financial instruments, currencies and commodities, with a view to, by applying analytical techniques, predicting future price movements. *See* fundamental analysis.

term (of a capital instrument) The period from the date of issue of the capital instrument to the date at which it will expire, be redeemed, or be cancelled (FRS 4).

total shareholder return Combined capital gain plus dividend income received by an investor over the investment period.

transaction exposure Susceptibility of an entity to the effect of foreign exchange rate changes during the transaction cycle associated with the export/import of goods or services. Transaction exposure is present from the time a price is agreed until the payment has been made/received in the domestic currency.

translation exposure Susceptibility of the balance sheet and income statement to the effect of foreign exchange rate changes. *See* foreign currency translation (Chapter 3).

treasury bill Short-term money market instrument issued, used to supply the government's short-term financing needs.

treasury management Corporate handling of all financial matters, the generation of external and internal funds for business, the management of currencies and cash flows, and the complex strategies, policies and procedures of corporate finance (Association of Corporate Treasurers). *See* Figure 4.3.

uncertainty Inability to predict the outcome from an activity due to a lack of information about the required input/output relationships or about the environment within which the activity takes place.

value-added tax (VAT) Tax on consumer expenditure, collected on business transactions and imports. VAT paid by all entities on inputs may be reclaimed or set against output VAT collected.

value-based management Management team preoccupation with searching for and

FIGURE 4.3 RELATIONSHIP OF THE TREASURY AND CONTROL FUNCTIONS

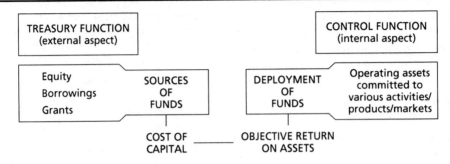

implementing the activities which will contribute most to increases in shareholder value.

venture capital Specialised form of finance provided for new companies, buy-outs and small growth companies which are perceived as carrying above-average risk.

warrant Financial instrument that gives the holder the right to purchase ordinary shares (IAS 33).

weighted average cost of capital (WACC)
The average cost of the company's finance (including equity, debentures and bank loans) weighted according to the proportion each element bears to the total pool of capital.
    Weighting is usually based on market valuations, current yields and costs after tax.

Example

Capital	Market Value	Rate
Equity	$8M × 10% =	$8M
Debt	$4M × 8.45% =	$338M
Total	$12M	$1,138M

Weighted average cost 9.483%
($1.138 million/$12 million)

    The weighted average cost of capital is often used as the measure to be used as the hurdle rate for investment decisions or as the measure to be minimised in order to find the optimal capital structure for the company. *See* cost of capital.

working capital cycle The period of time which elapses between the point at which cash begins to be expended on

the production of a product, and the collection of cash from the purchaser.

write-down A reduction in the recorded value of an asset to comply with the concept of prudence. The valuation of stock at the lower of cost or net realisable value (SSAP 9) may require the values of some stock to be written down.

writing down allowance A tax allowance, related to a firm's capital expenditure, which reduces profit subject to taxation.

yield curve A diagrammatical representation of the relationship between interest rates and the maturities of a similar set of securities. An upwardly sloping interest rate curve indicates that interest rates increase as security maturities lengthen. This might indicate that investors are averse to the increased uncertainty associated with future investment, and/or that there is an expectation that interest rates will rise in the future.

Z score A single figure, produced by a financial model, which combines a number of variables (generally financial statement ratios), whose magnitude is intended to aid the prediction of failure, that is a Z score model may predict that a company with a score of 1.8 or less is likely to fail within 12 months. Individual companies are scored against this benchmark.

zero coupon bond A bond offering no interest payments, all investor return being gained through capital appreciation.

Appendix

International Financial Reporting Standards

International Accounting Standards (IASs)

International Financial Reporting Standards (IFRSs)

IAS 1   Presentation of financial statements

IAS 2   Inventories

IAS 7   Cash flow statements

IAS 8   Accounting policies, changes in accounting estimates and errors

IAS 10   Events after the balance sheet date

IAS 11   Construction contracts

IAS 12   Income taxes

IAS 14   Segment reporting

IAS 16   Property, plant and equipment

IAS 17   Leases

IAS 18   Revenue

IAS 19   Employee benefits

IAS 20   Accounting for government grants and disclosure of government assistance

IAS 21   The effects of changes in foreign exchange rates

IAS 23   Borrowing costs

IAS 24   Related party disclosures

IAS 26   Accounting and reporting by retirement benefit plans

IAS 27   Consolidated and separate financial statements

IAS 28   Investments in associates

IAS 29   Financial reporting in hyperinflationary economies

IAS 30   Disclosures in the financial statements of banks and similar financial institutions

IAS 31   Interests in joint ventures

IAS 32   Financial instruments: disclosure and presentation

IAS 33   Earnings per share

IAS 34   Interim financial reporting

IAS 36   Impairment of assets

IAS 37   Provisions, contingent liabilities and contingent assets

IAS 38   Intangible assets

IAS 39   Financial instruments: recognition and measurement

IAS 40   Investment property

IAS 41   Agriculture

IFRS 1   First time adoption of International Financial Reporting Standards

IFRS 2   Share-based payment

IFRS 3   Business combinations

IFRS 4   Insurance contracts

IFRS 5   Non-current assets held for sale and discontinued operations

IFRS 6   Exploration for and evaluation of mineral resources

Notes

1. IASs not noted above have either been withdrawn or replaced by IFRSs.
2. IASs 1, 2, 8, 10, 16, 17, 21, 24, 27, 28, 31, 32, 33, 39 and 40 were revised in 2004 as a result of the International Accounting Standards Board's Improvements Project.

Appendix

United Kingdom Accounting Standards

Statements of Standard Accounting Practice (SSAPs)

Financial Reporting Standards (FRSs)

SSAP 4 Accounting for government grants

SSAP 5 Accounting for value added tax

SSAP 9 Stocks and long-term contracts

SSAP 13 Accounting for research and development

SSAP 19 Accounting for investment properties

SSAP 20 Foreign currency translation (*superseded by FRS 23*)

SSAP 21 Accounting for leases and hire purchase contracts

SSAP 24 Accounting for pension costs (*superseded by FRS 17*)

SSAP 25 Segmental reporting

FRS 1 Cash flow statements (*revised 1996*)

FRS 2 Accounting for subsidiary undertakings (*amended 2004 by legal changes*)

FRS 3 Reporting financial performance

FRS 4 Capital instruments (*mainly superseded by FRS 26*)

FRS 5 Reporting the substance of transactions

FRS 6 Acquisitions and mergers

FRS 7 Fair values in acquisition accounting

FRS 8 Related party disclosures

FRS 9 Associates and joint ventures

FRS 10 Goodwill and intangible assets

FRS 11 Impairment of fixed assets and goodwill

FRS 12 Provisions, contingent liabilities and contingent assets

FRS 13 Derivatives and other financial instruments: disclosures (*mainly superseded by FRS 26*)

FRS 14 Earnings per share (*superseded by FRS 22*)

FRS 15 Tangible fixed assets

FRS 16 Current tax

FRS 17 Retirement benefits

FRS 18 Accounting policies

FRS 19 Deferred tax

FRS 20 Share-based payment (IFRS 2)

FRS 21 Events after the balance sheet date (IAS 10)

FRS 22 Earnings per share (IAS 33)

FRS 23 The effects of changes in foreign exchange rates (IAS 21)

FRS 24 Financial reporting in hyper-inflationary economies (IAS 29)

FRS 25 Financial instruments: disclosure and presentation (IAS 32)

FRS 26 Financial instruments: measurement (IAS 39)

FRS 27 Life assurance

FRSSE FRS for smaller entities

Notes

1. SSAPs not noted above have either been withdrawn or replaced by FRSs.
2. Full implementation of FRSs 23, 24 and 25 will be dependent on the implementation of FRS 26.

Index

Lightning Source UK Ltd.
Milton Keynes UK
UKOW02f2011110514

231451UK00010B/174/P